CULTURE SMART!
GUATEMALA

Lisa Vaughn

·K·U·P·E·R·A·R·D·

This book is available for special discounts for bulk purchases for sales promotions or premiums. Special editions, including personalized covers, excerpts of existing books, and corporate imprints, can be created in large quantities for special needs.

For more information in the USA write to Special Markets/Premium Sales, 1745 Broadway, MD 6–2, New York, NY 10019, or e-mail specialmarkets@randomhouse.com.

In the United Kingdom contact Kuperard publishers at the address below.

ISBN 978 1 85733 348 0

British Library Cataloguing in Publication Data
A CIP catalogue entry for this book is available from the British Library

Copyright © 2007 Kuperard
Revised 2008; third printing 2010

First published in Great Britain 2007
by Kuperard, an imprint of Bravo Ltd
59 Hutton Grove, London N12 8DS
Tel: +44 (0) 20 8446 2440   Fax: +44 (0) 20 8446 2441
www.culturesmart.co.uk
Inquiries: sales@kuperard.co.uk

Distributed in the United States and Canada
by Random House Distribution Services
1745 Broadway, New York, NY 10019
Tel: +1 (212) 572-2844   Fax: +1 (212) 572-4961
Inquiries: csorders@randomhouse.com

Series Editor Geoffrey Chesler
Design Bobby Birchall

Printed in Malaysia

Cover image: Boats on the shore of Lake Atitlán. *Corbis*
Images on pages 17, 18, 58, 59, 63, 65, 66, 69, 71, 72, 73, 75, 85, 86, 94, 98, 100 (embroidered and painted work by Lucy Reyes), 101, 116, 126, 127, and 128 by permission of the author
Images on pages 13, 74, 125, and 129 by permission of INGUAT

About the Author

LISA VAUGHN is an American social psychologist. While gaining her Ph.D. from the University of Cincinnati, she trained in group interaction and relationships, organizational development, teacher-learning processes, and women's studies. Applying these disciplines to cultural studies—especially with Latino populations—she developed and led university study abroad programs to Guatemala from 2001 to 2005. She has lived and traveled in Guatemala for extended periods over the last six years, and has adopted a Guatemalan Mayan son. She is currently Associate Professor of Pediatrics at University of Cincinnati College of Medicine.

The Culture Smart! series is continuing to expand.
For further information and latest titles visit
www.culturesmartguides.com

The publishers would like to thank **CultureSmart!**Consulting for its help in researching and developing the concept for this series.

CultureSmart!Consulting creates tailor-made seminars and consultancy programs to meet a wide range of corporate, public-sector, and individual needs. Whether delivering courses on multicultural team building in the USA, preparing Chinese engineers for a posting in Europe, training call-center staff in India, or raising the awareness of police forces to the needs of diverse ethnic communities, it provides essential, practical, and powerful skills worldwide to an increasingly international workforce.

For details, visit www.culturesmartconsulting.com

CultureSmart!Consulting and **CultureSmart!** guides have both contributed to and featured regularly in the weekly travel program "Fast Track" on BBC World TV.

contents

contents

Map of Guatemala

introduction

The largest and most populous of the Central American countries, Guatemala is famously a land of contrasts and contradictions. It has great physical beauty, with ancient Mayan ruins, volcanoes, lakes, and rain forests, and a conglomeration of diverse peoples and cultures held together by fierce national pride and love for a country they want to improve.

Guatemala is unique in Central America in that more than half its population is of Mayan Indian origin. Today it is a combination of ancient Mayan heritage, Spanish colonialism, and Western influences, mainly from the United States. There has been an increase in tourism since the 1996 peace accords between the government and leftist insurgents ended a brutal thirty-six-year civil war.

Although the Maya may appear to be quiet and submissive, their colorful costumes, markets, and fiestas tell a different story. Most think of themselves as *indígenas* first and Guatemalans second, and are committed to safeguarding their Mayan identity, traditions, and customs.

In addition to the Mayan and Ladino peoples, there are two small ethnic groups, the Xinca and the Garífuna. Each group has its own cultural, social, linguistic, and economic characteristics.

Despite their horrific history and frequent disappointment in their governments, the Guatemalans remain hopeful for a better life. They are a vibrant and resilient people, sustained by their strong family relationships, who are committed to staying positive and looking ahead. Visitors will find them welcoming and friendly.

Culture Smart! Guatemala provides an introduction to the complexities of Guatemalan society. It shows how history has shaped the values and attitudes of today. It describes different aspects of Guatemalan life, including home, family, religion, festivals, typical food, and business practice. It offers key insights into the mind-set of the people, and practical advice on how best to behave in different situations and avoid cultural misunderstandings.

For a rewarding and enjoyable visit to Guatemala, forget your schedule and allow yourself to go with the flow of "chicken buses" and long conversations in the streets. Be prepared to meet and talk to Guatemalans from all ethnic groups and imbibe their rich culture. The more you immerse yourself in the country and the people, the more you will be enchanted. You will want to return, over and over again!

Key Facts

Official Name	República de Guatemala (Republic of Guatemala)	
Capital City	Ciudad de Guatemala (Guatemala City)	Population approx. 4 million
Major Cities	Guatemala City, Quetzaltenango, Antigua, Chichicastenango, Puerto Barrios, Escuintla	
Area	42,042 sq. miles (108,890 sq. km)	About the size of Tennessee
Terrain	Mostly mountainous with narrow coastal plains and rolling limestone plateau	Mountains include volcanoes, some of which are active
Climate	Tropical; hot and humid in the lowlands; cooler in the highlands	
Currency	Quetzal (Q) which divides into 100 centavos; named after the national bird, the quetzal	1 U.S. dollar = Q 7.6 1 Euro = Q 9.6
Population	12,728,111 (2007 estimate)	
Ethnic Makeup	Ladino and European, c. 40%; Mayan, c. 60%; Indigenous non-Mayan, 0.2%; other, 0.1%	

Language	Spanish 60%; Amerindian languages 40%	23 officially recognized Amerindian languages
Religion	Roman Catholic; Protestant; indigenous Mayan beliefs	
Government	Constitutional democratic republic with an elected president serving a four-year term	Unicameral Congress of the Republic. The president is both chief of state and head of government.
Media	The main TV channel is Canal 3. More than 300 cable operators, plus several evangelical channels. Several commercial and government-owned radio stations, plus evangelical stations	Main newspapers include *Prensa Libre, elPeriódico, Siglo Veintiuno,* and *La Hora*; popular press includes *Al Día* and *Nuestro Diario*
English Media	English-language newspapers are limited; some weekly editions published in English	U.S. cable channels are widely available.
Electricity	110 volts, 60 Hz A/C	European plugs need adaptors.
Telephone	The country code is 502.	To call abroad, dial 00 followed by the country code.
TV/Video	NTSC system	
Time Zone	GMT minus 6 hours (Central Standard Time)	

chapter one

LAND & PEOPLE

GEOGRAPHICAL SNAPSHOT

Guatemala, the northernmost of the Central American countries, is approximately 42,042 square miles (108,890 sq. km), making it about the size of the state of Tennessee, or of Ireland. It shares borders with Mexico and Belize to the north and northeast, Honduras and El Salvador to the east and southeast, and stretches from the Pacific Ocean to the Gulf of Honduras on the Caribbean Sea.

Three tectonic plates on the earth's crust meet in Guatemala, and there are many volcanoes in the mountainous areas, some of which are active, and occasional violent earthquakes. The short Caribbean coastline is susceptible to hurricanes and other tropical storms. The country consists of three main regions: the temperate rolling central highlands, with the heaviest population; the fertile tropical areas along the Pacific and Caribbean coasts; and the tropical jungle in the northern lowlands known as El Petén, which contains the famous Mayan site of Tikal.

The capital, Guatemala City, has a population of about 4 million people. Other towns and cities include Escuintla, Cobán, Huehuetenango, Quetzaltenango, Antigua, Chichicastenango, and Puerto Barrios. In 2007 the population was about 12.7 million, and the annual growth rate about 2.2 percent.

Guatemala is divided into twenty-two administrative *departamentos*, each of which has its own distinct cultural heritage and traditions. For instance, Huehuetenango—sometimes referred to as the "back door" of Guatemala because political leaders would often flee through it to Mexico to escape political strife—is the most ethnically diverse department, with seven languages spoken. Within it sits the municipality of Todos Santos, in the Cuchumatàn mountains, reachable from Paquix only by a gravel road. Todos Santos is home to the Mam-speaking

Mayas, and is said to have one of the most magnificent views in all of Central America. Also in Todos Santos, visitors will see an impressive display of traditional clothing. The men wear distinctive red and white striped pants with black woollen breeches and beautifully embroidered shirt collars. The women wear dark blue skirts and intricately designed purple blouses, or *huipiles*.

The department and municipality of Quetzaltenango—or Mayan Xelaju, shortened to Xela—is the second-largest city in Guatemala, and is predominantly Mayan. Mayan culture is often celebrated amid the remaining colonial buildings. It attracts many foreigners who want to study Spanish in a less touristy location than Antigua.

An even greater contrast can be seen in Lívingston, in the Izabal department, which can only be reached by boat from Puerto Barrios and is home to the Garífuna people—sometimes called the Black Caribs. The Garífuna are descendants of Amerindians and Africans, who originally were thought to be shipwrecked slaves from Nigeria who swam to shore and sought protection from the Caribs on the island of Saint Vincent. Lívingston has a tropical, Caribbean feel, and drumming and reggae rhythms can be heard throughout the town.

El Petén is located in the far north of the country. The area is covered by rain forest and is home to the Mayan ruins of Tikal.

Guatemala City, the modern capital, is the hub of Guatemala, where all flights come into and go out of the country.

DEPARTMENTS OF GUATEMALA

Alta Verapaz	Jalapa
Baja Verapaz	Jutiapa
Chimaltenango	Quetzaltenango (Xela)
Chiquimula	Retalhuleu
El Petén	Sacatepéquez
El Progreso	San Marcos
El Quiché	Santa Rosa
Escuintla	Sololá
Guatemala (Guate)	Suchitepéquez
Huehuetenango (Huehue)	Totonicapán
Izabal	Zacapa

CLIMATE

Guatemala has been described as "The Land of Eternal Spring." This name comes from the tapestry-like countryside, the year-round, springlike, moderate climate, and the vibrant colors of Mayan weaving.

There are two seasons—the dry season, from November (inland) or January (along the coast) to April; and the wet season, from May to October (inland), or December (along the coast). The coasts are hot and humid, with heavy rain during the wet season, although there is some decrease in humidity during the dry season. During the wet season it stays damp, with rain storms sometimes occurring daily. The highlands have less rainfall and are cooler at night.

Temperatures vary with altitude, ranging from an annual average of 77° to 86°F (25° to 30°C) on the coast, to 68°F (20°C) in the central highlands, and 59°F (15°C) in the higher mountains.

It is coolest during December and January, and in some areas there may even be snow on the mountain tops. Overall, Guatemala enjoys warm or hot days and cool evenings year-round.

THE CULTURAL DIVIDE BETWEEN MAYA AND LADINOS

Guatemala is home to the largest group of indigenous peoples within Central America. They are collectively referred to as the Maya (or the Maya or Mayan Indians). Westernized Maya and *mestizos* (mixed European and indigenous ancestry or assimilated Amerindian) are known as

"Ladinos," or locally as *Guatemaltecos*. The name
"Ladinos" was originally used to identify Spanish-
speaking Mayan Indians who provided labor and
overseeing of the plantations and were supposed
to keep the Maya in line. Later, Ladinos began to
acquire land and wealth, and today the term has
become chiefly a description of the national
culture of Guatemala, but still distinguishes it
from that of the true Mayan Indians.

Among the Maya, there are at least twenty-
three different ethnic or language groups. The
largest group is the K'iche' (estimated at about
887,000 people), followed by the Mam and
Kaqchikel (estimated to be some 440,000 people
in each group). Depending on how you classify
the Maya—whether they wear the traditional
dress (*traje*) or have abandoned it for a more

urbanized lifestyle, or by primary language spoken (a Mayan language or Spanish)—it is estimated that from 44 percent to as much as 65 percent of the Guatemalan population are indigenous Maya.

Certain areas of Guatemala are highly populated by the Maya. For example, Alta Verapaz is almost 100 percent Maya, and Sololá and San Marcos are about 80 to 85 percent. Today, the Maya are struggling to retain their cultural and ethnic identity and have organized various cultural activist groups in order to preserve their culture (such as, for example, Aso Trama Mayan women's weaving cooperative). Locally, Mayan activists call this *el movimiento Maya* (the Maya movement), while others have referred to it as Maya nationalism, the pan-Maya movement, and the Maya revitalization movement. Other groups in Guatemala include the Xinca, who are indigenous non-Maya, and the Garífuna, who are African-Guatemalans living on the Caribbean coast of the country with an ambiguous history regarding their origin.

The Maya are the largest American Indian group in North and Central America. Today, most Maya, about 5 million, live in Guatemala. The rest live in southern Mexico, Belize, and the western parts of El Salvador and Honduras. Strictly speaking, the term "Maya" refers to a historic grouping of languages, much like the Romance languages; today the word has come to represent the ethnic rights movement of the Mayan people in Guatemala. Whether a person is Maya or Ladino really depends on self-identification. Most Guatemalans actually have a mix of Mayan and Spanish bloodlines, with a few "purebloods" at each end of the continuum.

Most Ladinos refer to themselves simply as "Guatemalans" and generally live in urban centers, although there are poor, rural Ladino villages. Ladinos tend to dress in North American or European style, speak Spanish, and typically reject their Mayan heritage, regarding it as inferior.

Those people who identify themselves as Maya consider themselves the heirs of ancient Mayan civilization, speak a Mayan language, live in rural Mayan communities, eat traditional foods, and typically wear traditional dress, although this has been abandoned by some, especially men. The indigenous Maya have been considered inferior since colonization by the Spaniards, and ethnic discrimination based on this classification has been profound.

A BRIEF HISTORY

Very little is known about the region that is now Guatemala prior to the Maya civilization. The earliest inhabitants of the Americas are thought to have crossed the Bering land bridge to Alaska from Siberia during the Fourth Ice Age. If true, this would explain why the indigenous Amerindian populations seem to have some Asiatic features.

The earliest recognizable culture in the Guatemala area dates from around 10,000 BCE. The Clovis people were big-game hunters, living at the end of the last Ice Age, whose finely worked flint and obsidian tools have been found in the Guatemalan highlands.

The Early Maya Pre-Classic Period (c. 1800 BCE–250 CE)

Mayan civilization flourished in Guatemala during the first millennium CE. Then, mysteriously, it declined. Exactly what happened and why the Maya disappeared from various parts of Guatemala, Mexico, and Belize is unclear.

From excavations of ancient sites, we have learned that the early Maya settled in the central lowlands of the Petén between 2000 and 1500 BCE. The development of pottery and architecture in the Middle Preclassic period (c. 1000–300 BCE) shows the influence of the large Olmec civilization that originated in Veracruz, Mexico. From about 1 CE, in the Late Preclassic period (c. 300 BCE–250 CE), there was an explosion of Mayan culture in Guatemala with the building of pyramids and temples at Tikal, Uaxactún, and other cities in the Petén and around the country. One of the greatest pre-classic Mayan cities is

Kaminaljuyu, near Guatemala City. Later Mayan civilizations were noted for great cultural achievements, including hieroglyphic writing, knowledge of astronomy, architecturally designed cities, painted temples, stone monuments erected to honor important people, and other artistic forms such as painted ceramics and carved jade.

MAYAN ACHIEVEMENTS

Before the Spanish conquest, Mayan civilization dominated Central America. This was an extremely sophisticated and complex culture, with noteworthy achievements in architecture, agriculture, calendrics, astronomy, writing, and religion.

The ruins of the Mayan sites testify to the grandeur and impressiveness of the Mayan

civilization. One visit to Tikal is all one needs to understand the scale of their architectural greatness. Mayan architecture was based on pyramidal bodies with elaborate, lengthy staircases and incorporating wide-open spaces, the positioning often based on astronomical observations.

In agriculture, the Maya moved away from slash-and-burn methods to more refined techniques of terracing, drainage, and irrigation, which improved the fertility of the soil and the retention of needed water. They are credited with domesticating corn, and consequently are sometimes referred to as the "the people of the corn." The Maya also discovered vanilla beans, *frijoles* (beans), *chicle* (chewing gum), tobacco, and chocolate, among other medicinal products.

The Mayan people were obsessed with time. They developed elaborate calendar systems using astronomy and mathematics to understand and predict future events. The basis of calculation was a numerical system based on the number 20—and deities were assigned to represent the numbers one to  twenty in the calendrical system. The Mayan calendar had three distinct counting systems depending on the type and reason for the date. The 260-day sacred round calendar was used for timing rituals and ceremonial events. The civil calendar, the *haab*, was composed of 365 days and approximated to the solar year. The Long Count calendar, the most famous of the three Mayan calendars still used today by some, was for marking the passing of history. The current period of the Long Count calendar is supposed to end on December 10, 2012, which Mayan diviners see as an extremely important date, the beginning and end of an era.

In astronomy, the Maya were interested in the solar year, the lunar cycle, and movements of the planets. They were able to calculate all of these with astonishing accuracy compared to current calculations. They developed a highly sophisticated and artistic hieroglyphic writing, which in its style and use of pictures distinguishes it from other cultures of ancient Mesoamerica.

Alongside the development of sciences and architecture, the Maya had an elaborate theory of the origin of the world, the shape of the universe, and the deities living in it. Mayan cosmology is characterized by balance, layers, and opposites, and they believed in cycles of creation and destruction. According to the Maya, the earth is a flat surface with four corners each associated with a particular color (yellow for south; white for north; red for east; and black for west) and the color green at the center. They thought of the flat earth as the back of a giant crocodile relaxing in a pool of water lilies, and the sky as a double-headed serpent. They believed that there were many layers in the sky and that the four corners of the sky were supported by four trees of different colors and species (sometimes depicted as four extremely strong gods, called *bacabs*) with a great Ceiba (silk cotton) tree at its center. Above the sky existed a heaven composed of thirteen layers, each with its own god. In this conception, the top layer was overseen by a type of screech owl, the *muan* bird, and the gloomy underworld (*xibalda*) of nine layers was seen to be the destination after death.

The Maya believed in more than 160 deities, each of whom had variable manifestations (opposite sex, underworld counterparts, different ages, and so on). There is some evidence of a single supreme deity called Itzamná. A patrilineal line of Mayan priests were in charge of the calendars, festivals, ceremonies, rituals, divination, healing, writing, and learning. During most rituals, Maya engaged in bloodletting of themselves and their captives in order to anoint religious articles and as an offering to the gods.

"For the Maya, blood sacrifice was necessary for the survival of both gods and people, sending human energy skyward and receiving divine power in return. A king used an obsidian knife or a stingray spine to cut his penis, allowing the blood to fall onto paper held in a bowl. Kings' wives also took part in this ritual by pulling a rope with thorns attached through their tongues. The blood-stained paper was burned, the rising smoke directly communicating with the sky world."

("Mystery of the Maya," Nancy Ruddell et al, 1995. Canadian Museum of Civilization: www.civilization.ca)

Animal sacrifices and later human sacrifices were often performed as offerings to the gods. Incense was (and still is) almost always burned during Mayan rituals. Today, many Maya believe that the surrounding mountains are the equivalent of their ancient temple–pyramids where deities dwell, and for this reason, traditional shamans still pray at mountain shrines. There is also a continuing belief in the spirits of the forest and evil winds that can provoke illness and disease in the world.

The Classic Maya Period (c. 250–900 CE)
According to many archaeologists, Mayan culture was at its finest during this period. This was when the Maya developed the famous Long Count calendar and a recognizable form of writing. There was a marked increase in temple, altar, and monument construction and increased military conquest.

At the apex of Mayan society was the semi-divine person of the king, and below him a large, sophisticated royal court. Nobles ran smaller fiefdoms on his behalf, and a wealthy upper class surfaced due to the growth in long-distance trade. Status was displayed by jewelry and adornment. One of the most valuable commodities was chocolate: cocoa beans were used as currency, and the nobility drank the cocoa! At the base of society were the peasants who worked the maize fields and lived from the forests.

The Maya seemed to organize themselves with and trade among a federation of city-states, each with their own religion and culture. Warfare became common, with these city-states vying for power.

The Maya in Decline

After about 830 CE, the elaborate construction and material advances came to a halt. Although the reason is not known, there are many theories about what caused the decline of the Mayan population. Some believe that the great Maya city-states succumbed to the general conflict and disorder common throughout Mesoamerica; others that a peasant revolt may have broken out in response to the growth and unreasonable demands of the ruling elite. Some scholars point to overpopulation and a demand for increased food production, and the subsequent loss of soil fertility and environmental problems connected to the need to feed the growing population. Epidemics, widespread illnesses, droughts and other natural disasters may also have contributed to the decline and collapse of the Mayan cities.

By about the tenth century, Mayan culture began to die out in many of their previously well-populated areas in Guatemala. As the Maya abandoned their city-states, the majority moved to northern Belize, the Yucatán Peninsula, and the Guatemalan highlands to the south, where they developed small rural villages with terraced farming and irrigation. Today, this area of Guatemala still has standing ruins and monuments from the Classic period and the indigenous people are proud of their living Mayan traditions.

Preconquest: The Highland Tribes

Toward the end of the thirteenth century the Toltecs, an extremely militaristic tribe from northern Mexico, invaded the central Guatemalan highlands and dramatically changed the Mayan way of life. They created a much more secular and aggressive society based on military rule. The Toltecs as the ruling elite of the area founded a series of competing empires around Guatemala that began the fragmentation of the Maya into distinct tribal groups. The largest of these empires was the K'iche', who were dominant in the central area of Guatemala and later expanded their power base by conquering less powerful tribes. In 1475 when Quicab, the great K'iche' ruler behind the conquest, died, the empire suffered from lack of authority and power. For the next fifty or so years, all the tribes continued to be in conflict and fought over inadequate resources and the lack of available land.

The Spanish Conquest and Colonial Rule

The Spanish arrived in Guatemala to find much chaos and crisis, which they were able to exploit to their advantage. The Spanish adventurer Pedro de Alvarado had taken part in the conquest of Mexico with Cortés. He was dispatched from Mexico with an army of Spaniards and Mexican Tlaxcalans, who had allied themselves with Cortés during the Mexican conquest. Alvarado arrived in Guatemala in 1523 and quickly became known as one of the most evil, cruel, and rapacious *conquistadores* of his time. On a quest for gold and other profitable goods, Alvarado defeated most of the major Maya tribes in Guatemala; only the ferocious Achi in the Verapaces— known as the Land of War (Tierra de Guerra)— held his armies at bay. This area was eventually won over by Dominican missionaries led by Bartolomé de las Casas, the first Christian activist for the rights of native peoples, and earned its name of Verapaz ("true peace").

On his hunt for treasure and riches, Alvarado traveled to Peru, then back to Guatemala, and then was called in to quell a revolt in Mexico, meeting his death after being crushed by a horse that slipped and fell on top of him.

"Rotten Wood"

"Guatemala" comes from the word *quauhtemali*, which meant "rotten wood" in the Mexican Tlaxcalan language. The Tlaxcalan Mexicans who came to Guatemala with Alvarado were said to have found an old rotten tree near the seat of the Kaqchikel, one of the main Mayan ethnic groups located at Iximché.

The conquering Spaniards seized the Maya's lands and set up the *encomienda* system, forcing them to work the land that they had previously owned, and to pay the new Spanish owners with crops. The return payment was Christian teaching. During this time the Maya were treated like slaves, and thousands died from Western diseases against which they had no immunity. In order to limit the growing independent power of the *encomienda* owners, the kings of Spain regrouped the scattered Mayan communities into Spanish-style towns and villages (*pueblos*), each of which had a church and a marketplace at its center. This organization of *pueblos* aided the Catholic Church in the spreading of Christian doctrine, while the villagers served as a convenient labor force and source of taxation for those in power. Many Maya fled into the mountains to escape enslavement in the *pueblos*.

It was at this time that each Mayan village developed a distinctive style of dress with particular colors and symbols woven into their traditional clothing. Some believe that the Spanish used the traditional costume (*traje*) as a means of control, to keep the Maya in their specific villages, while others argue that the *traje* naturally developed within each village as an expression of Mayan creativity. The reality is probably somewhere in between, with the Spanish having some influence over the symbols introduced into the textile designs and the Maya developing their own designs within the villages. Later, during the recent civil war, the Guatemalan army did in fact use traditional dress as a means of control, in order to identify who belonged to which village.

Although this was not part of the Spaniards' plans, the Maya began organizing themselves politically and socially as villages at the beginning of the nineteenth century, and found ways to maintain their traditions alongside the newer Catholic power structures. Two centuries of colonial rule completely restructured the Guatemalan way of life, creating new cities, imposing the Catholic faith, reshaping the economy, based on exploitation of the indigenous Maya, and establishing a racist hierarchy with a small, extremely wealthy ruling class at the top.

Independence and the Coffee Boom

The Spanish grew disappointed with their conquest of Guatemala, perhaps because it did not turn out to be a source of great mineral wealth, as had been the case in Mexico and Peru, proving better suited to agriculture. Then, in the early 1800s, Spain became preoccupied with domestic matters. Napoleon's invasion of the Iberian Peninsula in 1808, and the adoption of a liberal constitution in Spain in 1812, led to reform in the Spanish colonies as well. These changes, combined with the increased burden of taxation to fund the war effort, led to the growth of independence movements in the New World. Continuing political turmoil in Spain would eventually result in the loss of her colonies.

In Central and South America there was a growing conflict between the liberals (in favor of a secular and more egalitarian state) and the conservatives (supporting the Church and the Crown), which resulted in several declarations of independence for Guatemala.

The first declaration of independence from Spain occurred on September 15, 1821, and September 15 still celebrated today as Guatemala's Independence Day. Guatemala was briefly annexed by Mexico and then in 1823 gained its second independence as it became part of the United Provinces of Central America, a republic and federation made up of Guatemala, El Salvador, Honduras, Nicaragua, and Cost Rica, with a federal government seat in Guatemala City. There were numerous revolts and general discontent among the Maya about their living conditions. One peasant rebellion in particular, headed by Guatemala's Rafael Carrera, led to the overthrow of the federal government and federation. Guatemala's bitter war against the federation resulted in the establishment of an independent republic in 1847.

The liberal opposition had been gaining momentum against the conservative rulers, and in 1871, under the leadership of Rufino Barrios, it launched a Liberal Revolution that

modernized Guatemala by
improving the trade system
and introducing new
manufacturing plant and
crops, especially coffee. This

coffee boom ultimately reshaped the
country, giving rise to a tremendous increase in
coffee exports, the establishment of a national
bank, development of ports, and extension of the
railway network. The Maya were forced into
labor on the coffee plantations and lost all their
remaining land, which was confiscated by the
government for coffee plantations.

The Banana Empire

After Barrios was killed in 1885 while fighting for a
unified Central America, Manuel Estrada Cabrera,
an authoritarian ruler who supported big
businesses, assumed dictatorial power in
Guatemala. Cabrera is noted for having the longest
one-man rule in Central American history. He was
instrumental in encouraging additional railway
expansion and foreign investment, in particular
with the U.S.-based United Fruit Company, which
monopolized business with the planting of
bananas in Guatemala.

With the election of Jorge Ubico as president in
1931, the United Fruit Company became the

dominant force in Guatemala, with even more power than the government; it invested great amounts of capital in the country, bought significant shares in the railroad, electric utility, and telegraph companies, and owned over 40 percent of the land. The company was sometimes referred to as *El Pulpo* (the Octopus), because of its pervasive influence and control.

Ubico ruled the country with an iron fist. He suppressed all political and intellectual opposition and continued to exploit the indigenous Maya, subjecting them completely to the state. He introduced an anti-vagrancy law that required Maya to carry a passbook proving they had worked 100–150 days a year, without pay, on the large estates or on public projects implemented by him. Without this proof, they could be put in jail, or worse. These laws reinforced the superiority and dominance of the Ladinos.

Ubico came to be quite paranoid, and developed an obsessive identification with the military during his thirteen-year reign in Guatemala. It is said that he saw himself as the reincarnation of Napoleon, and kept pictures of Napoleon around himself. He had a large spy network, was heavily guarded, and severely punished any dissent by incarceration or putting to death. As Ubico's regime grew more repressive, student and labor demonstrations and revolts increased. In 1944, he was forced to resign by the October Revolutionaries, a group of disenchanted military officers, students, and professionals, following the example of other popular uprisings against dictatorship in Central and South America at the time.

The "Ten Years of Spring"
After Ubico's overthrow, a provisional government ruled the country for almost two years. In 1945, a progressive and democratic intellectual, Juan José Arévalo, was elected president. As a former professor, he was able to institute social, educational, and health reforms and was instrumental in giving rights back to the Mayan people. His presidency started "The Ten Years of Spring," a period of free speech and political activity, attempts at land reform, and an ethos of progress across the country.

The next president, Jacobo Arbenz, continued in the same vein by taking on land reform and the biggest business monopoly in Guatemala, the United Fruit Company. Arbenz instituted the 1952 Law of Agrarian Reform, by which unused or state-owned land would be distributed to the landless. This infuriated the United Fruit Company (and the U.S.A.'s other commercial interests in Guatemala), long accustomed to doing as it pleased under previous governments in Guatemala, leading it to spread rumors of Communist infiltration in the Guatemalan government. These ultimately persuaded the Eisenhower administration and the CIA to orchestrate a CIA-led military coup to overthrow Arbenz.

Military Rule

Colonel Carlos Castillo Armas, who was responsible for the toppling of Arbenz, became president in 1954. He began to persecute and outlaw Communists, and in 1957 was assassinated, which brought a period of violence and unrest. Left-wing political activity continued to be suppressed for more than three decades. Many leftist organizers and nonpolitical Maya were killed during this unstable time. In 1960, a group of junior military officers, inspired by the Cuban Revolution, tried to overthrow the government, but failed. This group formed the base of the guerrilla movement that fought the Guatemalan government for the next thirty-six years. The army rose in power and became the dominant force in politics. The fighting between the left-wing guerrillas and the right-wing, U.S.-supported army and military government of Guatemala led to major violence and economic decline.

The worst of the bloodshed occurred when retired General Efraín Ríos Montt was president. He came into power in 1982 following a coup d'état and introduced a scorched-earth policy, part of a counterinsurgency campaign that—in the search for guerrillas and to eradicate any support they might find in the countryside—

resulted in the massacre of entire Maya Indian villages. During Ríos Montt's brief presidency, many thousands of civilians, usually unarmed Maya, were killed, tortured, and mutilated. Although violent executions, tortures, and forced disappearances were carried out by both sides, the majority of the atrocities were committed by the government-run military and the civil defense patrols under the military's control (estimated to be 93 percent of the violations).

It is estimated that some 626 Mayan villages in the highlands of Guatemala were destroyed, and approximately 100,000 Mayan Indians lost their lives through brutal means at the hands of the Guatemalan military. At the same time, numerous Mayan women and girls were raped and murdered, and many Maya fled to the mountains and jungles or went into exile in neighboring countries, especially Mexico, where many still live today. Some describe this violent history as genocide, the attempted eradication of the Mayan people. A K'iche' woman, Rigoberta Menchú, survived among the deaths of many family members. She gives an account of what happened to her and her community during the Civil War in her book *I, Rigoberta Menchú*. In 1992, she won the Nobel Peace Prize for her work for social justice and the rights of indigenous peoples.

The 1970s were a terrifying time for most Guatemalans, especially for those who publicly opposed and exposed repression and advocated reform. There are numerous reports of university student kidnappings and mutilated dead bodies found on the campus of the University of San Carlos, which had become a free-thinking intellectual center for protests and demonstrations against human-rights violations.

Return to Democracy

Ríos Montt was ousted by his defense minister, General Mejía Victores, in a coup in 1983. An amnesty was declared for the guerrillas and a new constitution was adopted in 1985. The constitution established an independent judiciary and a human rights ombudsman, and made way for Vinicio Cerezo Arévelo to be elected president—the first democratically elected president since 1966. Cerezo tried to end political violence and establish the rule of law, confining the military to providing security for the state. Although there was a decrease in violence and the economy improved at the beginning of his presidency, he did not prosecute human-rights violations vigorously, and he failed to deal with major problems such as infant mortality, illiteracy, poor health and social services, and resurgent political violence involving both the army and the guerrillas.

In 1991 Jorge Serrano Elías was elected president, the first civilian to succeed a previous civilian president. Under Serrano civil unrest grew. He suspended the Constitution, dissolved Congress and the Supreme Court, and censored the press, incurring both domestic and international opposition, and most foreign aid was frozen. Serrano was deposed and a return to constitutional rule was promised by Congress.

Congress then elected Ramiro de León Carpio as president, which gave much hope to the country as he was previously the human rights ombudsman. He hoped to put an end to government corruption and violence, but this hope was short-lived as human-rights violations continued and many communities took the law into their own hands because they perceived the government to be failing.

Toward Peace

Despite the issues in De León's administration, the peace process took on new life, especially when the United Nations became involved. Agreements were signed on human rights, indigenous rights, resettlement of displaced persons, and historical clarification. The rebels agreed to a ceasefire.

Alvaro Arzú followed De León in the presidency and concluded the peace negotiations. In December 1996, with the support of the United Nations, the government signed peace accords with the leftist insurgents, the Unidad Revolucionaria Nacional Guatemalteca (URNG), thus ending the thirty-six-year civil war in Guatemala. The peace accords called for a reduction in size of the Guatemalan army and the demobilization of the rebel forces. Arzú and his administration also took steps to reduce military influence in civil affairs and improve human rights.

Alfonso Portillo was elected to office beginning in January 2000, and promised to uphold the peace accords, reform the military, and investigate human-rights violations. Portillo was criticized by many because of the continued influence of Ríos Montt (then the head of Congress) in his decisions. Scandal, corruption, a faltering economy, and crime plagued most of Portillo's presidency.

The Twenty-First Century
In early 2001, public support for the government reached a record low as most Guatemalans had given up hope of a non-corrupt government. Although some progress had been made on human-rights issues, many problems were left untouched or not dealt with adequately. In 2001, Guatemala found itself confronting many challenges, including a high crime rate, continued human-rights violations, and government and public office corruption. In the summer of 2003, there were violent demonstrations in Guatemala City, with Ríos Montt's supporters demanding his return to power by calling for an overturn of a ban that would allow him to run for president even though he was a former coup leader.

In November 2003, Óscar José Rafael Berger Perdomo of the liberal reform GANA political party was elected president after a runoff vote against Álvaro Colom. This election was significant because there was a higher voter turnout than ever before, and because the electorate decisively rejected the former dictator Ríos Montt, despite his attempts to secure victory through bribery, vote buying, and intimidation.

In the fall of 2005, Hurricane Stan hit Guatemala, causing serious flooding and leaving many Guatemalans dead.

EMIGRATION

One consequence of the years of violence and war that destroyed hundreds of villages is the large emigré population of indigenous Maya and poor Ladino Guatemalans in Mexico, other parts of Central America, and the United States. Although some may have sought political asylum, the majority have left Guatemala because of their dire economic circumstances. It is estimated that about 60 percent of Guatemalans in the United States are without proper documentation. Guatemalans do not have Temporary Protected Status in the United States, which would prevent deportation to their home country during times of unrest. Approval rates for Guatemalan asylum applications in the United States increased from about 2 percent in the early 1980s to about 18 percent ten years later.

THE ECONOMY

The Guatemalan economy is dominated by the private sector and is based primarily on agriculture. Although it is the largest in Central America, there has been unequal distribution of land and wealth, and uneven development, with overdependence on foreign investment and a few agricultural exports—coffee, bananas, and cotton.

Guatemala has the highest Gross Domestic Product of the region, and the poorest record in Central America for illiteracy and infant mortality. It has the lowest average infant birth weight, the lowest ratio of doctors per patient, and the lowest percentage of children who are in school; these rates are worse for Maya than for Ladinos. The World Bank has reported that the indigenous people in Guatemala are the poorest of the poor.

There is a wide gap between the rich and the poor; the wealthiest 10 percent of people receive approximately half of all income in the country and about 80 percent of the population live in poverty, with about 66 percent of those people living in extreme poverty. More than 60 percent of the land is owned by less than 2 percent of the population. Wealthy landowners have always used cheap labor supplied by the Maya, and forced labor continued until the signing of the peace accords in 1996. Today, the Maya still work under harsh conditions, earning meager wages.

Diversification

In the 1980s agricultural exports were diversified to include cardamom, beef, sugar, and a greater variety than before of fruits and vegetables. Guatemala is now the world's largest cardamom producer.

Simple Solution

Guatemala is the fourth-largest producer of macadamia nuts in the world. Growing macadamia nut trees is preferential to the "slash-and-burn" agriculture (cutting trees and burning dried brush, which in the long term depletes the soil) that is common across the country, because the trees replenish the soil and their leaves take up carbon dioxide while releasing oxygen. There is an experimental macadamia nut farm, the Valhalla Project, outside Antigua.

In the 1990s, agricultural exports still accounted for at least 25 percent of the GDP and offered employment for more than half of the population. During the mid-1980s, sweatshop industries, mostly in garment manufacturing, were encouraged and created some 80,000 low-paid jobs. In the past few years exports of textiles and clothing have increased. In 2000, Guatemala, along with El Salvador and Honduras, signed a free trade agreement with Mexico for the purpose of stimulating the economy.

In 2000–2001, tourism became the country's largest earner, while the industrial sector grew steadily. This included drink and food production, and the manufacturing of rubber, textiles, paper, and pharmaceuticals.

For twenty-five years or so, economic development was held back by civil war, several major natural disasters, and low prices for agricultural and clothing exports. The economy has

grown more steadily in recent years. Guatemala's largest trading partner is the U.S.A, followed by El Salvador, Honduras, Mexico, and some E.U. countries, notably Germany and Italy. Guatemala is a member of the Central American Common Market, and in 2005 it ratified the Dominican Republic–Central America Free Trade Agreement (DR–CAFTA) and the U.S.–Central America Free Trade Agreement (CAFTA).

GOVERNMENT AND POLITICS

Guatemala is a constitutional democratic republic, with independent executive, legislative, and judicial branches of government. The executive is composed of the president, the vice president, secretaries of state, cabinet ministers, and vice ministers. The legislative body is the Congress, which has 158 deputies who are directly elected for four-year terms.

The judiciary is composed of the Corte de Constitucionalidad (Constitutional Court), the highest court in the land, and the Corte Suprema de Justicia (Supreme Court of Justice), which is the highest court of appeal in the country. There are also appeals courts, civil courts, and penal courts. Specialist courts deal with labor disputes or disputes of administrative litigation, conflicts of jurisdiction, military affairs, and other related concerns that are not governed by the ordinary courts. Trials are public, and defendants have the right to counsel, are presumed innocent until proven guilty, and can be released on bail.

Both the president and the vice president are elected by popular vote and can serve only one four-year term. The presidential elections of November 2007 were won by Álvaro Colom

Caballeros of the center-left UNE political party (see opposite) with nearly 53 percent of the vote. The president is both the head of state and prime minister, and commander-in-chief of the army. People who have been involved in a takeover or a coup d'état are ruled ineligible for the presidency, although the former dictator Ríos Montt challenged this law in the 2001 elections.

The twenty-two departments each have a governor who is appointed by the president, and the municipalities are governed by popularly elected mayors or councils.

For such a small country, Guatemala has many political parties, although political power has mostly been due to the personal influence of the leader rather than that of any political organization. These are some of the better-known parties.

- Frente Republicano Guatemalteco (FRG: Guatemalan Republican Front, conservative, right-wing), the party of José Efraín Ríos Montt.
- Gran Alianza Nacional (GANA: Grand National Alliance, liberal, leftist reform), the alliance of the former president Óscar Berger, which includes the smaller Patriotic Party, Reform Movement, and National Solidarity Party. GANA and FRG currently hold 37 seats in Congress.
- Some of the older parties that have been in Guatemala for over forty years are Movimiento de

Liberación Nacional (MLN: Movement of National Liberation, militantly anticommunist and right-wing) and Democracia Cristiana Guatemalteca (DCG: Guatemalan Christian Democracy).

- The left-wing guerrilla movement is housed under an umbrella organization founded in 1982 called the Unidad Revolucionaria Nacional Guatemalteca (URNG: Guatemalan National Revolutionary Union) and, as a political party, currently holds two seats in Congress.
- Several new political parties have been formed in the last few years. Chief among these is the center-left social-democratic Unidad Nacional de la Esperanza (UNE: National Unity of Hope), which holds 48 seats in Congress.

The flag of Guatemala includes a quetzal, the national bird, and a scroll inscribed with "Libertad 15 de Septiembre de 1821," which refers to independence from Spain.

GUATEMALA TODAY

Having emerged from its long, brutal past, Guatemala is concerned with creating a secure society, replacing paramilitary violence and authoritarian rule once and for all with a peaceful and socially participative government. Efforts have been made to increase tourism, and more recently attention has been focused on regional development and economic integration.

Guatemala receives donor support from the United States and other countries such as France, Italy, Spain, Germany, and Japan, who have all increased development project financing since the signing of the peace accords in 1996. Adequate relationships are maintained within Central America and with the United States; however, political violence and government corruption scandals continue to put a strain on these relationships.

People have become increasingly frustrated and concerned about the economy and the security situation. Poverty continues to be endemic, almost 50 percent of infants suffer from malnutrition, there are high illiteracy rates, and only a small percentage of Guatemalans enter high school.

In recent years there has been an increase in gang-related violence, unemployment, and the continued marginalization of indigenous groups. Violent crime is fuelled by poverty, the availability of weapons, the legacy of societal violence, and dysfunctional law enforcement and judicial systems. In December 2006, a United Nations backed commission was established to investigate organized crime and murders in Guatemala, which the authorities believe is linked to drug smuggling in transit to the United States. U. N. officials say that, with this new commission, they hope to solidify Guatemala's democracy and criminal justice system through the exposure and dismantling of organized criminal groups.

Álvaro Colom, the first social democratic president to be elected since Arbenz, has undertaken to reduce crime, tackle poverty, increase economic growth, and promote cultural diversity and tolerance. He is one of the few non-Mayans to be ordained as a Mayan priest, and his vice-president, Rafael Espada, is a cardiologist. The long-suffering Guatemalan people are desperate for honest, effective government. Remarkably, throughout their troubles, they have shown strength of character, resourcefulness, and even optimism about their future. There is great human potential in Guatemala waiting to be unleashed.

chapter two

VALUES &
ATTITUDES

The differences between the Maya and the Ladinos make it difficult to generalize about the Guatemalan population as a whole. There are really two distinct cultures in Guatemala—the dominant culture of the Ladino minority, and the abiding culture of the Mayan majority. Extremes of poverty and wealth contribute to the range of values and attitudes found among the people, as do the differences between rural and urban life. That said, the Guatemalan people can fairly be described as proud, strong, and vibrant. Visitors to the country are welcomed, and generally find a warm and friendly reception.

The influence of the Catholic Church is evident in many of the values held by people, although the Maya often mix ancestral religious beliefs with their Catholicism (see Chapter 3). Indigenous Guatemalans believe strongly in the value of their native culture, and are committed to safeguarding their heritage and maintaining their separate identity, which is rooted in Mayan traditions and customs.

IMPORTANCE OF FAMILY
AND COMMUNITY

In Central America generally there is an emphasis on family life and the community. It has been suggested that this focus on the collective rather than the individual may have originated in colonial times, when people preferred to solve problems within their communities rather than involve the Spanish authorities. In Guatemala, the Maya kept many indigenous beliefs and customs secret from outsiders. Today, the Maya still rely on their villages and communities for support and resources. Many Mayan communities have their own laws and a network of spiritual and political leaders who are effectively independent of the authorized government structures.

This emphasis on family unity (*familismo*) includes a strong sense of respect, loyalty, solidarity, reciprocity, interdependence, and cooperation among nuclear and extended family members. It is not uncommon in Guatemala to

see extended families living together and sharing responsibilities such as child care, the provision of food, and financial matters.

MAÑANA AND TIME ORIENTATION

Most Guatemalans operate within a "*mañana*" time frame. This means that punctuality is not a consideration, especially if something more important occurs. *Mañana* means "tomorrow," and indicates that time can be viewed flexibly. Rather than assuming that Guatemalans are irresponsible slackers, it is important to remember that, for most of them, time consciousness is simply not a top priority. These ideas about time also mean that the quality of an interaction is more important than how long it lasts. It is fairly common for Guatemalans to arrive thirty minutes or more late for an appointment or meeting. For them, 4:00 p.m. can mean any time between 4:00 and 5:00 p.m.—what's important is showing up, and the quality of the time spent together.

CARIÑO

Cariño means being affectionate with others, both physically and in speech. Guatemalans will demonstrate affection by a hug or a kiss on the cheek instead of a handshake, especially with friends and family. *Cariño* can also be noticed during conversations, such as in the touching of a person's shoulder or arm while talking. In the Spanish language, *ito* and *ita* are often added to the end of a noun or a person's name to denote endearment, and this is used frequently in Guatemala by all. For example, "*mi angelita*," "my little angel," is a term of endearment that is stronger than simply "*mi angel*," "my angel." In addition, much affectionate name-calling occurs among close friends. It is also very common to hear a person make a comment on another's appearance—such as *gordo/gordita/o* (fatty), *colocho* (someone with curly hair), or even *moreno/morenito* (brownie, darker skin)— whereby no insult is intended.

RESPECT, *SIMPATÍA*, AND NONCONFRONTATION

In general, Guatemalans like to pursue smooth interpersonal relationships and to avoid conflict and confrontation. Overall, they value indirectness, respect, and formality in interactions. Respect (*respeto*) is owed to individuals of greater status or power, such as the elderly, men, and wealthy people, and requires courteous and polite behavior. Typically, a person is much better received and more likely to have successful interactions when he or she demonstrates appropriate respect. Guatemalans tend to be sensitive to the opinions of others and are extremely proud, so it is important not to humiliate or embarrass anyone or cause them to lose dignity. If there is direct confrontation, many Guatemalans are likely to be offended, and may go as far as ending the friendship.

Simpatía, a related value, translates as "sympathy," but the meaning of the word in Spanish has more to do with pleasantness and congeniality, with an emphasis on interpersonal harmony and easy relationships. In Guatemala, direct argument or conflict is considered rude. Confrontation is not valued and most Guatemalans will avoid it at all costs, instead acquiescing or becoming overly agreeable.

In part, this desire to avoid confrontation may stem from the army's reign of terror in Guatemala, when it was better to answer questions vaguely and according to whoever was doing the asking rather than with a direct answer. This can still be seen today, especially in rural areas. A tourist might ask for directions, and a typical response would be, "Oh, that way," or "Who knows?" whether the person knows the right answer or not.

Ultimate Nonconfrontation

Heather, a businesswoman from the U.S.A. who had spent some time in Guatemala, became good friends with a Guatemalan Ladina woman, Edna, who worked in the criminal justice system. Edna recommended a lawyer friend to Heather for some assistance with legal matters, and Heather hired him. After a poor performance and some unprofessional behavior on the part of the lawyer, Heather began to question his ability to complete her case successfully. She casually mentioned her doubts to Edna. Edna became extremely offended, and although she never confronted Heather about this, she simply dropped her. Even though Heather tried to make amends, Edna would never speak to her again.

ATTITUDES TOWARD WOMEN

As elsewhere in Latin America, gender inequality and *machismo* are prevalent. *Machismo* involves extreme aggression in male-to-male relationships, and sexual aggression and contempt in male-to-female relationships. It is a way of controlling all or most aspects of a woman's life in order for the man to retain dominance. In Guatemala many men are conditioned to feel superior to women. They may engage in sexual harassment; they may have more than one wife or girlfriend, and they forbid their wives, sisters, and daughters to leave the house without their permission. A rural man may even dictate his wife's choice of birth control to ensure that her children are his.

It is a *macho* belief that education for women and girls should be discouraged so that the man of the house remains better educated, and thus more respected and honored within his community. It is common to see Mayan women trailing behind their husbands while walking down the street, and traditionally Mayan women are expected to cater to their husband's needs in any situation—if he has passed out drunk in the road, she is supposed to tend to him until he wakes up and is ready to go on. In general, men are expected to be the family providers and protectors, and are thought worthy of high respect.

Guatemalan women are thus caught "between a rock and a hard place," as they are both idealized and oppressed. They are placed on a pedestal for their superior moral and spiritual character, and mothers often seem to be in charge, but at the same time they are expected to submit to male authority. They are also expected to be both sexy and virginal at the same time. There are seemingly hundreds of beauty pageants in Guatemala, organized for every possible occasion—for sports teams, plantations, to preserve wildlife, and so on. It is common to hear men "catcalling" and hissing appreciatively as women walk down the streets, which may be part of *machismo*, but is also considered as a compliment. Men revere their mothers highly, and it is very offensive to insult a person's mother.

In recent years, there has been a shocking increase in physical assaults, rapes, and murders of Guatemalan women and girls. According to Amnesty International these brutal murders show

the pervasiveness of sexual violence, discrimination, and hatred of women in Guatemalan society. Some believe this violence is a distorted reaction to the sense of powerlessness felt by many men in the current social and political climate, others that it is a backlash against the upward mobility of women and girls. Compared to earlier times, more Guatemalan women are working, receiving higher education, and expressing themselves than ever before. However, these murders are evidence that *machismo* is alive and well and that women and girls are ultimately seen as disposable.

ATTITUDES TOWARD FOREIGNERS

Foreigners bring income, which is of course desirable, and Guatemalans are generally curious and welcoming to tourists visiting their country. However, there are unfortunate rumors in circulation about tourists that some indigenous people believe to be true. These include stories about visitors stealing Mayan babies, and also about the possibility of giving away children to tourists for a better life. Many Guatemalans have the perception that all Westerners are rich and have funds readily available for helping new friends. This view comes partly from the fact that tourists seem able to travel to Guatemala easily, some from long distances, meaning expensive plane tickets, whereas for many Guatemalans overseas travel is impossibly expensive. In addition, Guatemalans are constantly exposed to Western images of fashion and pop culture, which contributes to a belief that everyone in the U.S.A. and Europe leads a similar glamorous and luxurious lifestyle. Overall, despite the myths and false perceptions, foreigners can be expected to be greeted with warmth and hospitality and will find people eager to promote the charms and natural beauty of their country.

Assumptions About Foreigners

A U.S. director of a student mission program regularly took students to Guatemala to help build houses and, while they were there, take Spanish classes. One day she overheard the Guatemalan Spanish teachers talking about her: "She must be practically a millionaire because she is paying for all these students to come to Guatemala every year." They incorrectly assumed that the director was paying for every student when, in reality, they were each paying their own way to participate in the program.

Some Guatemalan men can be opportunistic in their friendliness toward foreign women, perhaps in the hopes of a marriage that would enable them to live abroad. Women travelers should be wary about men's advances and not always take them at face value. The increase in violence against Guatemalan women has been known to affect women travelers, although not to the same extent, and it is wise for women to use caution when traveling in the country. For most women travelers, however, the effects of the male chauvinist culture are generally annoying rather than threatening, as long as they are careful where they go and make sensible travel plans.

PREJUDICES

In general, the indigenous Maya are viewed as inferior, "second-class" citizens in Guatemala. You are likely to hear the racist term "*indio*" still used by Ladinos to refer to them. The Maya are more often found in menial, low-paid jobs (such as domestic service, manual labor, or selling their produce or handicrafts). It is very common to see a wealthy Ladino family with a Mayan domestic worker who is serving as nanny, cook, and housekeeper. Although there are black Guatemalans (the Garífuna) who live

predominantly on the east coast, there appears to be no overt prejudice against black people of any nationality. The main prejudice seems to be reserved for the Maya (*los morenos*—literally "the browns") from some Ladinos. This prejudice has been in place since the arrival of the Spanish and means that in the provision of services such as health and education the Ladinos and those of Spanish descent have almost always been favored. Prejudice does not seem to extend to foreigners, who sustain the much-needed tourist industry.

chapter three

RELIGION, CUSTOM, & TRADITION

Religion in Guatemala has changed and blended over the centuries, and continues to remain an important part of both Maya and Ladino culture. Guatemala is officially a Catholic country and has been this way since colonization began over five centuries ago. However, many indigenous Maya have held on to their traditional spiritual beliefs, and in the highlands traditional priests can be found who guard the secret rituals and customs of the Maya. Most of Guatemala's religion can be classified as syncretism, a mix of indigenous beliefs and customs and mainstream Catholicism. In addition, there are many Protestant groups and evangelical sects that have increased their numbers in the past twenty years or so.

THE CATHOLIC CHURCH
Christianity was introduced in the 1500s with the Spanish conquest of Guatemala. Sometimes by

imposition and sometimes by free will, Roman Catholicism in some form was adopted by most of the local population. The Catholic Church was extremely wealthy and powerful during this time and every *pueblo* had a Catholic church at its center. Today Guatemala is known as a Catholic country, although its constitution grants freedom of religion. Some 50 to 60 percent of Guatemalans identify themselves as Catholic.

Many of the Catholic churches are extremely interesting to view, with unique exteriors and vivid displays of saints within.

INDIGENOUS MAYAN RELIGION

A thousand years ago the Maya constructed pyramids, built city-states, and worshiped numerous gods. Society was agriculturally based, which resulted in the worship of nature and animals, and especially the sun. In fact, each Mayan person is thought to be born under the sign of a protective animal (*nahual*) to which certain personality traits and destinies are attributed. This *nahual* is believed to help them communicate with nature throughout their lifetime.

Remains of many ancient Mayan ceremonial sites still exist today, although many have been destroyed for various reasons throughout history. Some of the better-preserved and more elaborate sites, with temples, pyramids, and plaza remains, are found in Tikal, Uaxactún, and over the border at Palenque in Mexico. At the height of their civilization, the Maya developed their famous calendar system and used hieroglyphics to record their history and mythology. The Mayan religious belief system is called "*cosmovisión*," and emphasizes prophecy and the cyclical nature of history. The most inclusive creation writing is the *Popol Vuh*, also known as the Bible of the Americas. Written around the sixteenth century, clandestinely copied from older hieroglyphic books but using Roman letters, this K'iche' document describes the beginning of the Mayan people in four eras of creation and destruction, and includes descriptions of Pedro de Alvarado's conquest and Christianity.

Spiritual beliefs and traditions have contributed to the survival of much of the Mayan culture. In local Mayan villages there is a religious hierarchy of male officeholders. These men move to and from various posts that are grouped into *cofradías* (brotherhoods), each of which is responsible for the care and "housing" of a particular saint. Throughout the year of a post, the saint is kept safely in an elder member's home until it is time for it to take its place in a religious procession, when it is paraded through the streets and taken to its next home.

For traditional Mayan believers, native priests (sometimes referred to as diviners, or shamans, or *brujos*, literally "witches") address personal religious issues through communication with the gods and spirits. These Mayan priests are descendants of the ruling priestly elite of classic Mayan civilization. They preside over rituals that usually take place at a shrine, or a cave in the mountains, or an ancient Mayan site, where offerings of incense and alcohol are made. These priests are also thought to cast spells, predict the future, and communicate with the dead. For medical concerns, the Maya often go to *zahorines*, practitioners of traditional medicine, who are associated with the Mayan priests.

Traditional Mayan religion declined as a result of colonialism, the arrival of Catholic missionaries in the Mayan highland areas in the 1950s, Catholic reform movements, and the Protestant missionaries who arrived in Guatemala after the 1976 earthquake.

SYNCRETISM

Under Spanish rule, Mayan religion and rituals were prohibited. In some areas, the local people held on to their traditional beliefs and practiced their religion in secret. This resulted in a varying syncretic mixture of faiths, a coexistence and blending of traditional Mayan and Christian beliefs and rituals. This can still be seen in the fusion of Mayan deities and Christian figures; in some cases, Catholic saints and icons have taken the place of traditional gods and idols, with the basis of belief remaining in indigenous religion.

The religion of Guatemala is, however, officially called Catholicism.

One of the most interesting examples of syncretism is the worship of Maximón, or Saint Simone, in many Guatemalan villages. Maximón is a maize god, an anti-saint of sorts, who is known for his love of drinking and smoking. According to legend, Maximón was supposed to take care of the women while the men were out working in the fields. His way of taking care of them was to sleep with them, thus enraging their husbands, who cut off his arms and legs in revenge. Today, Maximón is represented by a dummy figure who  is dressed and cared for in various chapels or worshipers' homes. Local people come to ask for his help with problems caused by misdemeanors (such as that of a relative in jail, or an alcoholic uncle), bringing gifts of rum and cigars to appeal to him. Many Mayans believe that he can protect them from evil spirits, and help them in their quest for wives, jobs, and riches.

EVANGELICAL SECTS

Guatemala has seen the largest growth of evangelical Christianity in Latin America. According to the Evangelical General Council, the Alianza Evangelica, there are more than 19,000 Protestant churches in Guatemala representing more than ninety denominations, including Baptists, Nazarenes, and Guatemalan-created Pentecostal groups such as El Shaddai. The Assembly of God is the largest denomination, followed by the Church of God of the Complete Gospel. In recent years Protestant and Evangelical missionaries have been competing for followers. Many have brought hope and practical assistance to rural villages—building houses and helping in the provision of food, medicine, and education—and have gained many converts.

Some attribute the Evangelicals' success in Guatemala to their strong opposition to gambling, alcohol, and domestic violence—traditionally the Catholic Church has not interfered with pre-Columbian practices that do not conflict directly with the Catholic faith. They believe that Guatemalans are turning to these sects because they provide a sense of order, identity, and belonging that counteracts the instability that people have felt for many years. The Protestant Churches have traditionally been less tolerant of syncretic practices than the Catholics, and some Evangelicals insist that indigenous deities like Maximón should retire, viewing such syncretic beliefs and practices as satanic and growing out of witchcraft. It is believed, however, that indigenous members of Evangelical Churches still practice traditional Mayan rituals in secret.

The Maya, who believe strongly in their traditional practices, feel that by targeting them the Evangelicals are trying to take their culture away from them.

RELIGION TODAY

Worship takes many forms today in Guatemala, encompassing traditional Catholic services in modern and historical churches (the oldest church in Central America is located in Salcaja), outdoor

revivals, and preaching on the chicken buses. Typically at Evangelical services and revivals worshipers sing, dance, and wave their palms. Most revivals, which usually occur on Saturday evenings, have a loud amplified band that accompanies the singing. Songs and sermons in Spanish are punctuated by loud cries of "Hallelujah!" from the congregation.

It is very common to see ancient Mayan rituals being performed at ruined sacred sites throughout the country. Sometimes there are animal sacrifices, from which tourists are usually excluded.

Overall, some 50 to 60 percent of the population are estimated to be Catholic and around 40 percent are estimated to be Protestant, mainly Evangelical. The Mayan Spiritual Organization believes that some 40 to 50 percent of Mayans perform some type of native ritual, although only about 10 percent are publicly open about their practices.

Other religions in Guatemala include the Church of Jesus Christ of Latter-day Saints (Mormons), Jehovah's Witnesses, Judaism, Islam, and followers of the Indian spiritual leader Sri Sathya Sai Baba. The Mennonites also have a following in Guatemala, and are recognized by their distinctive minimalist appearance and way of life, including their famous baked goods and dairy products.

FESTIVALS AND HOLIDAYS

The indigenous *fiestas* are some of the most distinctive in Latin America, with most honoring a particular saint. They generally include costumes and traditional masks, and can be very noisy, with loud firecrackers and merrymaking along with heavy alcohol consumption. Each town and village has at least one day a year that is devoted to

celebrating the local saint, with some areas
extending the party by a week or two around the
special day. In mainly Ladino areas, most *fiestas*
have religious processions, in which the patron
saint is carried through the streets, as well as beauty
contests, with contestants usually riding on the
backs of cars or trucks, marching bands, merengue
and salsa dancing at nights, and fairs containing
rides, games, and food and drink stands.

In the Mayan populated highlands, typical
fiestas include traditional costumes, dances, and
music, all with a pre-Columbian influence. There
are crowds, much noise, and alcohol
consumption. Some of the more important
festivals are marked by a special element, such
as the huge kites at Santiago Sacatepéquez, the
religious processions in Antigua, the horse race
in Todos Santos Cuchumatán, or the skull bearers
of San José.

Guatemalans Love Firecrackers!

Don't be alarmed if you are woken up by what sounds like gunshots as early as 5:00 in the morning. Guatemalans use firecrackers (*cuetes*) to celebrate anything and everything! Expect to hear early morning firecrackers for birthdays, holidays, anniversaries, and really anything else worth celebrating. December seems to be an especially fervent firecracker month, with the morning blast occurring almost every day.

In addition, most of the major cities and *pueblos* have other fairs and festivals throughout the year, where the area takes on a general festive atmosphere of partying, parades, and exhibitions ranging from traditional dances and customs to small games, amusements, and rides.

Piñatas—brightly colored containers full of candy and toys—are very popular at parties, especially for children's birthdays. They can be purchased at grocery stores, outdoor markets, and even at local homes from people who make

them and hang them from their front rafters to sell. The *piñatas* have an opening so that all kinds of little treats can be put inside. At the birthday party, children are blindfolded and hit the *piñata* with a stick until it bursts open, all gathering up the candy and prizes.

PUBLIC HOLIDAYS

January 1 New Year's Day

January 6 Epiphany

March/April Semana Santa. The four days of Holy Week leading up to Easter

May 1 Labor Day

June 30 Army Day (anniversary of the 1871 Revolution)

August 15 Guatemala City fiesta (Guatemala City only)

September 15 Independence Day

October 12 Discovery of America (only banks are closed)

October 20 Revolution Day

November 1 All Saints' Day

December 24 (from noon) Christmas Eve

December 25 Christmas Day

December 31 (from noon) New Year's Eve

Street processions are a common sight. On saints' days people carry large statues of the saint through the streets. Funerals are usually conducted in a street procession with people walking and carrying the casket. There are many local beauty pageants, where the contestants ride atop cars and are paraded through the streets before the winner is announced.

Important holidays in Guatemala include Easter week, particularly in places like Antigua; All Saints' Day, occurring on November 1; and Christmas.

MAKING FRIENDS

Guatemalans are very sociable, and start building the majority of their friendships at a young age. Extended family members provide important and key relationships and it is common for extended families to get together frequently, maybe two or three times a month, to eat, drink, enjoy the party, and catch up on the latest news.

For foreigners, it is easy to meet Guatemalans at Spanish schools, at work, or on nights out at bars and discos. You can expect them to be very friendly, but it may be harder for you to form deep, long-lasting friendships. Remember that it takes time to build trust, and trust is at the heart of good relationships with Guatemalans.

Generally, close friends in Guatemala have known each other for many years and have virtually become assimilated into one another's families. Friendships also extend to distant relatives. It is fairly common to see cousins, aunts, nephews, and so on socializing and sometimes even living with another relative's family. Some Mayan Guatemalans view foreigners with suspicion, and, as we have seen, there are a number of myths about Westerners and their wealth or their behavior that can influence interactions. However, a persistent effort on your part can turn suspicion to trust and friendship.

As in many relationship-based societies, people often ask favors of their friends, and expect them to grant them. The underlying principle seems to be, "you scratch my back, I'll scratch yours." Because some Guatemalans have the perception that all Western tourists are wealthy, and they themselves have high levels of poverty, it is fairly common for a Westerner to be asked for money or other help by a well-intentioned Guatemalan friend. By the same token, foreigners can expect their Guatemalan friends to help them out in different ways, such as accompanying them while they travel, providing assistance with running errands, health needs, gift purchases, and so on.

Guatemalans may refer to foreigners in a joking way as "*gringos*," but this is not meant in a derogatory way. They refer to themselves as a "*Guatemalteco/a*" or more colloquially as a "*chapín/chapína*." Some young people are now wearing hats and T-shirts bearing the legend "100% Chapín."

Exchanging Favors

Two young women students from the U.S.A. came to Guatemala for the summer to learn Spanish and experience Guatemalan life. They wanted particularly to see the famous Tikal ruins, sample life in Lívingston, and travel all over the country. This would require long bus trips and take at least two weeks, and they were afraid to travel as women alone. They decided to ask a male Guatemalan friend if he would be willing to accompany them if they paid all his expenses. He obligingly arranged time off from work and joined them on the trip. The trio had a delightful time, and all returned highly satisfied with their exchange of favors.

HOSPITALITY AND THE VISITOR

As a people, Guatemalans are hospitable, polite, and accommodating, and tourists are generally appreciated as adding to the economy. Guatemalans like to give a good impression and will do so at all costs, even if it means hiding the reality of a harsh life. In Mayan communities, visitors may at first be treated rather distantly, but upon getting to know people and building up relationships, they can expect to be treated with warmth.

It is common to be invited to a Guatemalan home for lunch, the biggest meal of the day. This generally involves a large spread of food and lively conversation. Expect to be offered second and third helpings by the hostess—a common method of welcoming a visitor into the home.

True Generosity

A foreign exchange student from Europe and her family (a husband and two small children) had been living in Guatemala while she studied Mayan civilization at a local university for one semester. They were renting an apartment, but had to move out earlier than expected, and were set to stay the rest of their time in a hotel room. On learning this, a Guatemalan friend invited them all to live with her family (also a husband, two children, and a housekeeper) for the remaining month. Guatemalans will often go beyond the call of hospitality to help you out.

GIFT GIVING

In Guatemala the giving of gifts is one of the ways people maintain good interpersonal relationships. For example, if visiting someone's home for dinner, it is important to bring something small, such as wine or a bunch of flowers. Be sure to ask the florist which flowers would be appropriate, to avoid giving those specifically used for funerals— these are generally white. If you are invited for lunch, your hostess will be delighted if you bring a dessert. (See more on gift giving in Chapter 8.)

TABOO SUBJECTS

In general it is acceptable to talk about most subjects with Guatemalans, including potentially sensitive topics such as politics and religion; however, some of the less suitable subjects include Guatemala's violent history, which has touched almost every family in some way, and openly sexual topics. Religious affiliation, too, seems to cause some tension in Guatemala, especially if you are not Roman Catholic. Catholicism is the accepted religion and you will probably encounter the view that other religions are not as good, or not as important. For example, it is quite common to hear Catholics talking about "those Evangelicals," as if they were sinful, or less worthy than Catholics.

One major taboo is homosexuality, which is generally not accepted across Guatemala. Of course there are gay men and lesbian women there, but unless you are in certain circles within the larger cities, this subject will not be discussed openly among family and friends. Gay and lesbian couples tend not to be open about their sexuality.

LEARNING SPANISH

Guatemala is one of the most popular and economical countries for foreigners who want to study Spanish, and there are plenty of schools that have made this into a big industry. Some of the schools are well established, and some are relatively new, and may hold classes in the front room of someone's home. Antigua and Quetzaltenango are the two most popular cities with students, with numerous Spanish schools in each. Antigua has more tourists, while Quetzaltenango has fewer tourists and just as many schools. Many of these Spanish language schools can provide homestays with native Guatemalans, and offer field visits and adventure trips with guides.

chapter five

HOME LIFE

HOUSING

Houses in Guatemala vary according to social class, whether one is Ladino or Maya, and whether one lives in a rural or an urban area. Because the majority of Guatemalans live in some poverty, you will see a number of Ladino families living in what once was a beautiful colonial house that has now become run-down. Colonial houses in Guatemala typically feature an open central courtyard, with living room, dining room, and bedrooms leading off it.

The majority of urban middle-class Ladinos (shopkeepers, small business owners, teachers, doctors, lawyers, and so on), particularly outside the capital, are surprisingly poor by Western standards. Their homes tend to be inadequately built, run-down, and sometimes structurally unstable. Then there are the shantytowns of tin-roofed shacks attached to the cities, where displaced Maya and impoverished Ladinos live. There is, however, a small percentage of Ladinos

living in very nice colonial and Western-style homes, usually in the urban centers. There are luxurious vacation homes, usually owned by foreigners, available in tourist areas like Antigua and around Lake Atitlán.

Rural life is quite different, with widespread poverty affecting the indigenous communities of the countryside. Most rural poor live in primitive housing without indoor plumbing, and use communal washing areas for laundry and dishwashing and the rivers for bathing. Most of their houses are built of adobe (sun-dried bricks), although more recently concrete houses with roofs of aluminum or ceramic tiles have sprung up. The smallest may consist of only a single large room. Electricity reaches almost everyone, except in the most remote areas, and is used primarily for light, refrigeration, and television.

FAMILY LIFE

Daily life revolves around the family in
Guatemala. As we have seen, there is strong
loyalty within families, even for extended family
members. It is common to see large families living
in the same household or within the same block.
If family members don't live within a household,
they probably won't be far away. Guatemalans are
not likely to spend much "alone time" as they are
constantly socializing with family, extended
family members, and friends.

Godparents (*padrinos*) are an important part
of the family. Parents are said to be *espejos*
(mirrors) through whom children learn who they
are and what they can become. Children continue

to rely on their parents for advice and guidance
throughout their lives. Even if family members
don't particularly like one another, it is still

expected that they will spend time together, especially on holidays or for significant events.

Traditionally, Ladino families have been medium to large in size, perhaps with four to six children, and possibly with extra children of relatives, or an ailing grandparent, living within a household. Today, Ladino couples typically have two children simply because of economic constraints.

Within the Mayan culture, families are usually large and life is extremely traditional. Men wield authority in Mayan villages, and women are expected to run the home. Daily life revolves around the men tending the cornfields (*milpas*) and vegetable gardens while the women stay at home cooking, weaving, and looking after the children. Mayan women, however, do travel with children in tow to out-of-town markets to sell handicrafts, textiles, surplus vegetables, and fruits, and to trade for needed supplies.

Many Mayan women serve as *domesticas* (housekeepers) for Ladino families, even if the Ladino family is not wealthy. Some *domesticas* are provided with room and board for the week and may travel to their villages on the weekends. Others, with husbands and children of their own, may travel back and forth daily. These women cook and clean, and sometimes look after their employers' children. Overall, the *domesticas* are treated well by the Ladino families, although they are still viewed as inferior.

Traditional Guatemalan families are hierarchical, with special deference given to the elderly, parents, and men. The Guatemalan father is an authority figure and the mother is expected to be self-sacrificing for the family and obedient to her husband. Domestic violence is very common in Guatemala, with estimates as high as 90 percent. Generally, domestic violence is viewed by both men and women as an acceptable means of asserting male control within the household.

CHILDREN

Children are very important to Guatemalans—a household without children is thought to be lonely and sad. Guatemalan children are generally raised strictly and are expected to be obedient, but they are indulged when small, so they don't cry or complain too much. Generally, Mayan children are expected to contribute financially to the family as soon as they are capable. A very common sight in Guatemala is a young Mayan woman carrying her baby on her back, strapped on by a rectangular piece of material called a *tzute*. The baby stays on the mother's back while she works. It is not unusual to see Mayan children as young as five or six years old selling handicrafts to make money for the family. Ladino children are usually not expected to work until they are teenagers. Boys tend to be afforded greater freedoms, while girls are often quite restricted. Older children are expected to take care of younger siblings and older sisters are often seen serving as a substitute mother.

Many Guatemalan children of Mayan origin are given away for international adoption because their mothers cannot support them due to extreme poverty, and because many young women have children out of wedlock, which is generally viewed as unacceptable. There are also thousands (estimates are vague, but are in the range of 5,000 to 10,000) of "street children," mostly Mayan, living in Guatemala City and other cities. These children are either runaways or castaways from families too poor to feed them. The majority are homeless, and sleep on cardboard or sidewalks at night. During the daytime, they beg for money, scrounge food, and scavenge from dumpsters, and often spend hours high from sniffing glue or other inhalants, which are cheaper than most food. Many Ladino Guatemalans view the street children as a nuisance and worry only about the poor impression they make on tourists. There are very few shelters or organizations to help the children.

EDUCATION

Education is valued by most people in Guatemala and is generally seen as a way to better oneself. However, the education system is struggling along with very little financial backup. It is of poor quality, is concentrated in the cities, and has ethnic and gender inequalities. In addition, many Mayan parents do not believe in formal education for their children since the curriculum does not include information about their heritage and culture. This attitude results in low attendance, especially during the harvest period; high dropout rates; grade failures; and poor test scores in primary school. Within rural communities, schooling suffers because of the lack of schools in general and the children's involvement with farming.

The Maya have long been concerned that formal education in Guatemala erodes their cultural identity. After decades of campaigning, the Academia de Lenguas Mayas (the Guatemalan Academy of Mayan languages) was established to revitalize Mayan cultures and languages. The Academy has standardized the Mayan alphabet and this is taught in most indigenous primary schools today.

Ladino children in the cities may start attending preschool at three years of age. There are six grades of compulsory primary (*primeria*) school, covering the ages seven to thirteen. Attendance rates are low (about 40 percent) as enforcement is slack. Secondary (*secundaria*) school has two cycles: the basic secondary school from ages thirteen to sixteen, which results in a Diploma de Estudios; and "diversified" secondary school from ages sixteen to eighteen or nineteen, depending upon the specialization. After two years, the students take an exam for the Bachillerato de Ciencias y Letras, which is a prerequisite for university, along with an admissions exam for some universities. A three-year program in technical education leading to the Perito Comercial, Industrial, Agricola, Técnico diploma is also available at the secondary level. There are both public and private school systems in Guatemala, with most private schools being affordable by middle- to upper-class Ladino families.

For Maya children whose families want them to progress beyond the basic education available in the villages, there are either public schools or Catholic schools. Catholic-run boarding schools are the main source of further education for children from rural Mayan communities.

Higher education in Guatemala is provided by one state university (the Universidad de San Carlos de Guatemala) and several private universities. Instruction is in Spanish. The first level degree at university is the *Técnico* or *Diplomado*, and is typically awarded after two to three and a half years of study. The next level is *Licenciatura*, which is awarded after four to five years of study and submission of a thesis (medicine requires six years). The third stage is the *Maestría* and *Doctorado*. The *Maestría* degree is given after one to two years of further study after the thesis, and the *Doctorado* is awarded after two consecutive years of study following the *Licenciatura* degree and thesis submission in Law, Humanities, Education, Economics, and Social Sciences.

Illiteracy is a big problem in Guatemala. The literacy rate is about 71 percent overall, with far lower numbers within the Maya, especially of Mayan women (who have a literacy rate of approximately 30 percent).

More and more educated Guatemalans are learning English as a means to get ahead. English is often a required course in private schools, and there are after-school programs that offer English classes.

LA QUINCEAÑERA

La quinceañera, the celebration of a girl's fifteenth birthday, marking her passage from childhood to adulthood, is an important religious and social event in Guatemala. The celebration begins with a mass attended by the girl, her family, and her godparents. This is followed by a lively reception for family and friends, with music, food, and dance. Traditionally the girl wears a special dress for the occasion, typically an elegant ball gown. She receives special fifteenth-birthday presents, which may include religious jewelry, such as a cross, other jewelry, and religious objects (bibles, prayer books, and rosaries). There is a often a *quinceañera* doll to commemorate the event, which will become a keepsake. The guests are likely to be given memorabilia, such as ribbons bearing the girl's name and the date, to take home with them.

There are stores in the larger cities that specialize in suitable fifteenth-birthday gifts and party favors for the occasion.

COURTSHIP AND MARRIAGE

Since Guatemala is a Catholic country, the conduct of courtship, at least publicly, reflects traditional Catholic values. Brides are supposed to be virgins, and girls are therefore more strictly supervised in their dating and courtship. Boys, however, are expected to lose their virginity before marriage. Dating is important for young Guatemalans, and couples tend to meet in public parks or at the central square since there are not many places where they can spend time alone together. It is not unusual to see teenage couples kissing and caressing in the streets and other public places. Dating, like marriage, is ruled by

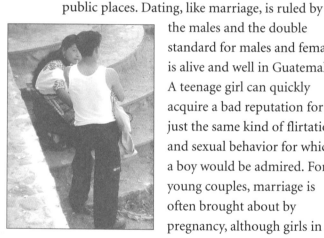

the males and the double standard for males and females is alive and well in Guatemala. A teenage girl can quickly acquire a bad reputation for just the same kind of flirtatious and sexual behavior for which a boy would be admired. For young couples, marriage is often brought about by pregnancy, although girls in general tend to marry young, at around seventeen years old. Sex education is not popular in Guatemala, and many parents avoid the topic with their children.

Weddings tend to be large and joyful, with many extended family members, including babies and children, and friends in attendance. There are flowers, dancing, and singing. In a traditional Guatemalan wedding, the bride and groom are tied together by a silver rope as a symbol of their eternal bond. Not only the bride wears white—even her bridesmaids and flower girls will be dressed in white gowns. Most Ladino weddings follow a Catholic ceremony, but many also include traditional, non-Catholic elements. The bride's and groom's godmothers often play an important role, offering their blessings. At Guatemalan weddings, it is common to see bell-shaped *piñatas* filled with raw beans, rice, and confetti.

Marriage remains extremely traditional in Guatemala regardless of social status. Men have the ultimate authority, and are expected to be the breadwinners for their families. Although divorce is legal, it is not very common because marriage remains the norm and the ideal. Parents support their children financially until they are married, and some newlyweds remain living with one set of parents for several years, perhaps until they have children.

Among the Maya, marriage customs vary according to the particular traditions of the village, but many villages expect the groom to pay the bride's parents a bride price. Historically, the groom would also work for his parents-in-law for a period of time decided upon by the bride's father. Traditionally, marriages were set up by a matchmaker, the primary goal being the procreation of large families. Some Mayan couples cannot afford a wedding so live together in common-law marriages.

DAILY LIFE

There are extreme contrasts in the standard and conduct of everyday life in Guatemala. Wealthy families who live in Guatemala City enjoy a cosmopolitan lifestyle similar to that in a European city. The daily life of the poor rural Maya remains very traditional, with the majority working in agriculture as subsistence farmers or day laborers and in the production of handicrafts.

The daily round for the majority of Guatemalans, whether Ladino or Mayan, starts early. In a typical Guatemalan family, the woman will wake at about 5:00 a.m. to begin household tasks such as washing clothes and preparing food. At around 6:00 a.m. she will wake her husband and school-age children and serve them breakfast. At 7:00 a.m., the father goes to work and the children to school. If the family has a *domestica* then she will go to the market, clean the house, and prepare lunch; otherwise the mother will do this work. At 1:00 p.m. school is over and most children come home for a big lunch. The remainder of the day is spent with the children doing homework and extracurricular activities or classes such as English, arts, sports, music, and math. Many families are heavy television watchers, especially in the afternoon and evening, although most families will only have one television in the house. Most children go to bed at 9:00 p.m. and the parents later, around 10:30 to 11:00 p.m.

In rural families, life revolves around agriculture, and the daily routine depends on the climate of the region. For example, in the coastal areas the men will wake up as early as 4:30 a.m. to begin work at 5:00 a.m. before it becomes too hot. The women mainly stay at home to care for the children and cook for the family; however, they will also do heavy labor when needed, such as climbing the mountains to cut and carry wood for the fires, washing clothes in the river, and carrying water for cooking and drinking. In rural areas, women accompanied by their children usually take lunch to their men working in the fields, and the family eats as a group.

Most shopping is done in the marketplace. The biggest market in Guatemala is in San Francisco el Alto on Fridays. Here anything and everything you want can be purchased, including food, clothing, and even livestock. Other famous markets include the Thursday and Sunday ones in Chichicastenango and the Friday market in Sololá. Almost every village has its weekly market day, when people come to trade their surplus produce and to socialize. On market days the plaza is full of activity, with people arriving in pickup trucks, on buses, by foot, and by donkey.

Bargaining is the name of the game. This is good-humored, and does not usually involve raised voices, unless there is a mishap, which generally seems to involve foreigners, with the foreigners doing most of the yelling.

There are large supermarkets in the cities, and if a family has easy transportation, their own car or a minibus, then they will shop at these large convenience stores, some of which have both food and housewares.

MEALS OF THE DAY

For extremely poor Guatemalans, the basic diet consists of corn, beans, and fruit.

A typical breakfast consists of mashed or refried black beans, tortillas, fried or scrambled eggs with tomato, onion, ham or sausage, and plantains. It is usually eaten between 6:00 a.m. and 7:00 a.m. In rural areas, families may have *atol* (a corn- or rice-based drink) for breakfast.

Lunch is the main meal of the day, and is eaten sometime between 12 noon and 2:00 p.m. It consists of soup, tortillas, meat, and several side dishes of vegetables and fruits.

Supper is generally a more modest meal, and may simply consist of leftovers from lunch. In the larger cities, people may go out to eat, typically between 7:00 and 8:30 p.m., and have a more substantial dinner.

At every meal, before eating, during eating if someone interrupts, and after everyone has finished eating, Guatemalans always wish each other "*Buen provecho!*," which means, roughly, "Good health!"

EMPLOYMENT

About 50 percent of the population of Guatemala are involved in agriculture and this percentage is even higher among the Maya. Thirty-five percent work in tourism services, and 15 percent in industry. Both at work and at home, there is a division of labor along gender lines, with men doing the more demanding manual and field work if there is a farm, and women doing more of the

household work, or service positions if they work outside the home. Generally, both Ladino men and women work outside the home. Mayan women also work outside the home, but this usually takes the form of selling produce or handicrafts at markets.

HEALTH SERVICES

Like the educational system, the Guatemalan health system is limited and inadequate. Hospitals and clinics are underfunded and understaffed. Only about half the population has access to health care. In the large cities, for those who can afford it, good quality medical care is available—there are public and private hospitals and some health centers. There is usually at least one pharmacy in the larger towns and cities. For minor health problems, it is common for a pharmacist to play a diagnostic role and prescribe medication, even antibiotics.

In rural areas, the health situation is worse, with some communities receiving no regular health care or health education at all. Folk healing and traditional medicine are commonly used. Most women in the cities give birth in hospitals, whereas women in rural areas are attended by a midwife in their homes.

DRESS

Rural villages are more conservative than the cities, with most locals wearing traditional indigenous dress (*traje*), which reflects the view that, especially for women, the body should be covered. In Guatemala City, other large cities, and popular tourist sites such as Antigua and Panajachel, a more Westernized and casual style of dress is common, although one often sees the Maya in

their indigenous clothing. Professional, white-collar workers dress accordingly, with men in suits, shirts, and ties, and women in suits, skirts, and dresses, with panty hose and almost always high-heeled shoes. Ladinos with less money often dress in secondhand clothing from the U.S.A., which they purchase in markets and shops specifically for this type of clothing.

Traditional clothing connects the Maya to their past and is also a major part of their present-day identity. It is the most visible manifestation of the Mayan philosophy and belief system. Each design is associated with a particular village, and more than a hundred and fifty Guatemalan towns are documented as having distinctly different *traje*.

Although many of the designs are dynamic, as generations of women have modified and customized the woven artwork over the years, the essential elements of the *traje* remain constant. The designs use combinations of colors, animal and plant motifs, human figures, abstract shapes, words, and even names. Many of the motifs are thought to predate the Spanish Conquest—examples are the commonly used sun, moon, and snake from classic Mayan art. The quetzal bird is one of the most pervasive symbols used in the textile designs. Today it is the national bird of Guatemala, but it dates to before the Conquest, when the quetzal was seen as the spiritual protector of the K'iche' kings.

The basic upper garment for women consists of a *huipil*, a loose blouse made from three separately woven panels. It is brocaded and embroidered with colorful designs and usually sewn up the sides to form armholes, with the seams being oversewn with ribbons or decorative stitching. With the *huipil*, women wear a skirt (*corte*) with a woven belt or sash (*faja*). This is the standard daily wear for most rural Maya women. For special occasions, ceremonial *huipiles* are designed even more elaborately, with symbolic motifs usually associated with the cosmos or cycles of time—these can take up to six months to weave.

In Nebaj, a town high in the Altos Cuchumatanes mountains, the women's *traje* is one of the most eye-catching in Guatemala and has won top awards in international pageants of traditional costumes. It consists of a red skirt with yellow stripes, a woven belt, a heavily embroidered *huipil*, an all-purpose shawl, and an elaborate headdress woven into the hair.

In contrast, the women of Santiago Atitlán wear a *huipil* of purple-striped white cloth embroidered with fanciful motifs and figures of animals, birds, and flowers. The most striking feature of their costume is the headdress, which is wrapped many times around their head to form a disklike shape. This is illustrated on the Guatemalan 25-centavo coin.

In San Juan Atitlán, another mountain village, both men and women are commonly seen in traditional *traje*. The men's *traje* is one of the most distinctive and elegant in Guatemala. They wear a red shirt (*camisa*) with a long squared-off collar, the ends of which are stitched to be used as pockets. Over the red shirt, a black or dark brown tunic (*capixay*) is worn and held in place by a sash. The pants are white and plain and the ensemble is usually topped off with a straw hat and a festively decorated shoulder bag (*morral*).

Women use a backstrap loom to weave their unique clothing, tapestries, and textile artwork. This simple apparatus consists of two bars of wood with lengthwise warp threads extended between them. The woof thread is woven with a shuttle that permits the incorporation of a wide range of effects not possible on a commercial loom. To use it, the weaver attaches one end of the loom to a house post or tree, and the other end to her hips or waist, and sits on the ground or stands, leaning back to keep the warp taut for weaving. This loom has been used in Guatemala for over four thousand years with little change in the technique. Although not without many challenges to its survival, this ancient art form is recognized as one of the few "living" artistic traditions still alive after more than 450 years of great challenges and changes. Weaving, now and in the past, reflects a great sense of cultural identity for the Maya. It is thought to have connections to the creation of the universe, and is considered by some to be carrying on the work of the gods.

chapter six

TIME OUT

Because of commitments to family and work, most Guatemalans do not have a lot of time for leisure activities as such. However, family gatherings and *fiestas* are frequent and much time is spent talking to neighbors. During the hotter months, you will see entire families at the public swimming pools and barbecuing. It seems that Guatemalans are always glad to find an excuse for a party—to celebrate birthdays, welcomes and farewells for visitors or extended family members living elsewhere, weddings, baptisms, church confirmations, *quinceañeras*, anniversaries—quite apart from the many holidays and *fiestas* in the villages and cities.

WHERE GUATEMALANS MEET UP

In the large cities there are all types of bars and cafés where people meet for drinks. There are many popular discos where friends meet to dance salsa, merengue, and combined versions of blended hip-hop with salsa and merengue. Cinemas are found only in large cities, and typically show only films produced in the U.S.A.

In all Guatemala's cities and towns, especially the smaller towns, the central square is of the utmost importance. This is the vital heart of the place, where people meet and stroll, and where weekly or monthly markets are held. The Sunday saunter through a city park or town center is a universal pastime. The verb for this particular activity is *dominguiar*, "to Sunday," which means to meander around in a leisurely, aimless fashion on a Sunday. Even at other times, it is common to see all ages "hanging out" in groups, sitting on the benches, on blankets, or on the park wall. Young people will meet up there for evening outings. The central plaza is also the site of most political demonstrations.

In the larger cities, there are shopping malls where Ladinos and Maya alike enjoy window-shopping and strolling. It is common to see entire families casually walking through the malls on weekend evenings.

FOOD
Guatemalan food can be categorized as typical Maya, urban Ladino, and African-influenced

Garífuna cuisine, although there are some standard dishes, such as *tortillas* and beans, that occur throughout the country. In general, the food in Guatemala is adequate, but it should not be the primary reason for a visit.

For the typical Mayan family, food comes from their own homegrown crops or what they trade at market. Maize is the primary staple, and every Mayan woman knows how to make *tortillas*— small corn pancakes made from ground maize flour, which are cooked on a clay platter (*comal*). These are usually flat and round, but can be shaped into all sorts of forms such as logs, balls, and so on. *Tortillas* are eaten at almost every meal, accompanied by some form of black beans— soup, refried paste, puréed, with rice, and so on. Vegetables are also common fare, especially squash, tomatoes, hot chilies, and hot peppers.

Speciality dishes eaten in the Guatemalan highlands include *pepían*, a unique chicken stew

flavored with pumpkin seeds, hot chilies, and tomatoes and *pinol*, a chicken-flavored corn mush. Other Mayan dishes include *caldos* (stews made with different types of meats), *fiambre*, which is a special salad of meats and vegetables served on All Saints' Day (November 1), and *mosh* (porridge of oats and milk eaten for breakfast).

For Ladino Guatemalans, the food is a combination of Mexican, U.S., and European cuisine, although many still eat traditional Mayan food as well. Steak, hamburgers, chow mein, rice, and fries are all common foods. Readily available are German-style sausages and Italian-style pizza and pasta. Ceviche is more common on the coasts. Some Ladinos, especially rural folks, commonly follow a Mayan diet primarily composed of *frijoles*, *tortillas*, cheese, cream, chili, and coffee. *Carne asado* (charcoal-broiled fillet of beef), *chicharrones* (fried pork rinds), *chiles rellenos* (meat-stuffed peppers), and *tamales* (little filled dough pies) are all widespread favorites.

Garífuna cuisine is more tropical in nature and has African roots. Bananas, coconuts, and seafood are commonly used in recipes in and around the coastal area of Lívingston. Fried plantains are also a well-known food across Guatemala originally made popular by the Garífuna.

DRINK

Coffee and tea are the most common accompaniments to meals, although soft drinks and juices are readily available as well. *Liquados* are popular, smoothielike drinks that are made with water, milk, or yogurt blended with fresh fruit (be sure to ask for *agua pura*, purified water, if ordering it with water). If you buy a soft drink or *liquado* on the streets or to go (*para llevar*—to carry, literally), you will usually be given a plastic bag with a straw and the drink inside.

Festive occasions call for beer; the two popular brands are Gallo and Moza. An indigenous drink made in the highlands is *Caldo de Frutas*, which is a drink of fruits fermented by soaking them in rum. You can drink the flavored liquid or eat the fruits. Quetzalteca is a popular and very inexpensive rum or "fire-water" that can be purchased at any small *tienda* (store) or gas station.

Both Ladinos and Maya are fond of alcohol. In fact, alcoholism has become a problem among Guatemalan men, sometimes leading to public disturbances, and has contributed to the breakup of families. Ladinos like a good party, and the men certainly like to drink a lot. A similar double standard seems to apply to women and alcohol as with sexuality. While it is permissible for Ladina women to drink, it is thought that this should be in limited quantities, and it is socially more acceptable if they drink something "light," such as wine or a flavored mixed drink, rather than beer or any hard liquor.

As we have seen, some Maya families have turned to evangelical religions that prohibit alcohol in order to combat the abuse and overuse of alcohol within their culture.

If you attend a special dinner party or celebratory outing, expect there to be drinking. In bars, it is typical to see groups of Ladinos (sometimes with tourists) purchase multiple, entire bottles of vodka, rum, or whiskey to share with the group. Another Guatemalan perception of Westerners, especially college students, is that both men and women drink lots of alcohol and engage in wild accompanying behavior when partying. Foreign women should use discretion with Guatemalan men when socializing at bars, especially if they are consuming alcohol.

EATING OUT

Restaurant fare in Guatemala will vary according to the size of the city or town. There is a distinction between a restaurant and a *comedor*, which is an inexpensive café serving simple food that is popular with locals. There are a number of

American fast-food restaurants in the cities
(McDonalds, Taco Bell, and Pizza Hut are the
most common) and, surprisingly, a growing
number of Chinese restaurants. In the larger
cities, good restaurants of all types can be found,
although the most expensive ones do not
necessarily have the best food or service.

Guatemala is a country of meat-lovers, and
vegetarians should be warned that there is not
much vegetarian fare. Chicken is a favorite dish,
and chicken restaurants are ubiquitous. The Pollo
Campero chain, for example, is so popular that
Guatemalans often transport large packs of Pollo

Campero chicken across the border to relatives
living in the U.S.A. *Churraso* (charcoal-grilled
steak), barbecued meat (often open air), and
chicharrones (pork crackling) are also Guatemalan
carnivore delights that can be found in
restaurants and at street vendors.

TIPPING

Good restaurants expect a 10 to 15 percent gratuity for service, especially from tourists—and an additional tip is left for the *marimba* (wooden xylophone) band if one is playing there. Tips are not usually included in the price of meals or other services and are not expected from Guatemalans, unless the restaurant caters primarily to foreigners. If the tip has already been included in the bill, it will appear as "*propina*" near the total.

There is a sales tax of 12 percent of the total amount of the purchase, and a hotel room tax, also 12 percent. Tips are appreciated by hotel staff, but are rarely given to anyone else, such as taxi drivers. However, if an exclusive arrangement is made with a taxi driver whereby only he is called on for services, tips may be given to maintain his willingness to pick you up at a moment's notice.

SPORTS AND EXERCISE

It is probably not surprising, given that it is a Latin American country, that soccer is the most popular sport in Guatemala. The game is almost a religion for boys and men, and is played in the farthest villages, in any location, whether there is a soccer field or not. Guatemalan males are active soccer players and enthusiasts from a young age. Guatemala City has the largest soccer stadium in Central America. It is typical during the World Cup, for example, for people to wake at all hours of the night to catch the scheduled game, regardless of who is playing. However, if a Latin American country is playing in the World Cup then Guatemalans will be as supportive as if their own country were playing.

Soccer apart, sports in general seem to be mostly the preserve of middle-class Ladinos in Guatemala, with the children starting to participate at early ages in after-school activities or clubs. The daily newspapers devote a full section to sports. Baseball, American football, boxing, and basketball are popular. There are bullfights annually in Guatemala City, featuring matadors from Mexico or Spain. Bicycling has also increased in popularity for both Guatemalans and tourists. Visitors to Guatemala can spend time hiking and climbing the volcanoes, or fishing on the coasts, and there is the possibility of white-water rafting.

PERFORMANCE ARTS

Guatemala, especially the cities of Antigua,
Guatemala City, and Quetzaltenango, is home to a
limited number of performing arts venues, which
are patronized mostly by upper-class Ladinos and
foreigners. There is a national symphony orchestra,
and national chorus, ballet, and opera companies, all
of which perform at the
National Theater in
Guatemala City. The
theater is not as well
developed, but there are
theater groups that
perform in larger cities.

   Garífuna music is highly popular in Guatemala,
and the *marimba*—akin to a wooden xylophone—
is the national instrument, played in religious
ceremonies and at social and community events
across the country.

SHOPPING FOR PLEASURE

Guatemalan crafts (known locally as *artesanía*) are
very popular with tourists. Each artistic tradition is
localized, with different regions, and sometimes
villages, specializing in particular crafts. These
handmade products are exquisite, with the most

well-known being the colorful woven textiles that are sold all over the world. Other local crafts include the wool and blankets of Momostenango, the reed mats made near Lago de Atitlán, and rope crafted in Cotzal and San Pablo la Laguna. Other villages have specialties in pottery or flowers. It is best to purchase Guatemalan crafts in their places of origin, both because the quality is likely to be better and because this ensures that the locals get more of the profit. However, good selections can be found in the local markets or in tourist locations. While you

are in Antigua, an interesting place worth a visit is a Mayan textile store and museum called Nim Po't, at 5a Avenida N. #29. This shop offers an array of contemporary and antique Mayan dress, including *huipiles*, belts, skirts, and hair ornaments, and Mayan handicrafts. It is also one of the places that carry paintings, calendars, and cards by the artist Claudia Tremblay, whose work captures the beauty and essence of the Mayan people.

For everyday shopping, you can find just about everything you might want at shopping malls, large chain grocery stores, or within towns at individual shops.

Worry Dolls

Guatemalan "Worry Dolls," made from leftover textiles, are known around the world. These tiny dolls are usually packaged six together in a small wooden box. Only about an inch (2.5 cm) tall, they are made by wrapping yarn or scraps of cloth around paper-wrapped wire. At bedtime, Guatemalan children confide their problems to their dolls, one at a time, and believe that the dolls will take their worries away while they sleep.

chapter seven

TRAVEL, HEALTH, & SAFETY

Although it is possible to travel to Guatemala by land via Mexico, the easiest and safest way is by air. There are direct flights to Guatemala City from many of the major cities in the U.S.A. From Europe, there are plenty of flights that stop in the U.S.A. and continue on to Guatemala, but it can be cheaper to fly into Mexico and travel to Guatemala on a smaller connecting flight (or by land, of course). In addition, there are plenty of package tours to Guatemala, especially for viewing the Mayan ruins, for bird-watching, and for hiking in the jungle. With a valid passport, citizens of the European Union, the U.S.A., Canada, and many other countries do not need a visa, and most visitors can stay in Guatemala as a tourist for up to ninety days.

GETTING AROUND

Once you are in Guatemala, you should carry your passport, or at least a copy of it, with you at all times, because you may be asked to show it.

The cost of living is quite low when compared to North America or Europe. The quetzal is the Guatemalan currency, although U.S. dollars and credit cards are accepted in many places.

In terms of traveling around the country, there are inexpensive in-country flights to Flores for trips into the Petén from Guatemala City.

By Bus

The majority of people travel by bus, and there are several options to choose from. There are private buses, called pullmans, which cover all the major routes in Guatemala. These buses are usually old Greyhound buses from the U.S.A., and they vary tremendously in their quality and comfort. Tickets can be bought ahead of time, and buses leave from their terminals. Many still pick up passengers along the way, especially if they are not full.

A cheaper, perhaps less comfortable, but more adventurous way of traveling is by *camionetas*—"chicken buses" to foreigners. These are old U.S. school buses that have been painted in bright, sometimes gaudy, colors, and decorated with names and pictures both outside and inside. The majority of the locals use these buses to most destinations and they are typically packed full,

with people standing in the aisle, hanging off the back, and sometimes on the top of the bus. Although uncomfortable, with seats intended for small children, full of noxious fumes, and driven at speeds that defy the curves of the mountain roads, *camionetas* provide a true taste of Guatemala, with vendors selling snacks and goods riding on board for short distances, on-bus preachers, loud music, and often livestock such as chickens (part of the reason for the name given them by tourists to Guatemala). Many of the pullmans and virtually all the *camionetas* have *ayudantes* ("helpers"—assistants to the drivers). These young men shout out destinations, alert the driver to oncoming vehicles while hanging out of the door, pack the bus until it cannot hold another person or bag, collect money from everyone by squeezing along the aisle, direct lost tourists in Spanglish, and climb atop the moving vehicle to arrange and retrieve the baggage.

In many of the larger cities there are minibuses that travel within the city for low fares, usually jam-packed with passengers. It can be a bit tricky to figure out the routes for these, but you can ask the locals who use them.

By Car

It is possible to rent a car in Guatemala but this can be expensive, and there is always an issue of security in terms of theft and vandalism. U.S. driver's licenses are accepted for a limited visit, and international driving permits for longer stays. Motorists use the right-hand side of the road, and speed limits are in kilometers, although they are rarely enforced. Seat belts should be worn at all times, and using a cell phone while driving is not permitted. There are no laws about child safety seats, and it would be best to bring your own.

Driving and traffic rules are viewed casually by Guatemalans. Speed limits, staying within lanes, and road signs are not usually observed. Many drivers will stick their hand out of the window to indicate that they are about to do something, but it is often unclear what they are going to do! Driving on curving, mountainous roads can be extremely dangerous, as cars and buses pass each other blindly. Many

roads contain large potholes, are dimly lit
at nighttime, and always seem to be
undergoing construction (that never
seems to be completed); there is the
added hazard of landslides. Do not
drive outside the large cities at
night because the risk of being a target of
crime is increasing, and also because it is difficult
to see where you are going.

It is possible to hitch rides, especially in
remote areas where people travel in the back
of pickup trucks.

Taxis

There are taxis in the main towns and the rates
are very reasonable, although it is important to
agree on a price before you get into the cab, as the
majority do not use meters. Many taxis and a few
minibus owners are often willing to negotiate
excursions for a fee, especially if there is a group
of people wanting to travel to a specific location.

Bikes and motorcycles can also be rented and
used for travel around the country. There are
ferry and boat services for crossing water, and
fares for these are usually negotiated much like a
taxi unless it is a specific regular service for
which there is a fixed price.

With all these methods of travel, it is essential that visitors do only what feels comfortable, and use common sense about their own safety when traveling to and from remote areas, or traveling at night.

WHERE TO STAY

There is a large range of accommodation, with varying levels of quality and price. The hotels in Guatemala can be referred to as *hoteles, pensiones, posadas, hospedajes*, and *huespedes*, and there is no real distinction based on name. In addition to hotels, there are guest houses, homestays, apartment rentals, and camping options. Electrical outlets are usually standard American outlets with a current of 110 volts, 60 Hz.

A word of warning. When using the bathroom in Guatemala, you are expected to put used paper in the trash can, usually placed next to the toilet. Only in the better hotels and restaurants is this not the case. It is also a good idea to bring at least one roll of toilet paper or some tissues along with you until you are settled somewhere, because you may not find any in public restrooms. If traveling by pullman or chicken bus, make sure you let the driver or his assistant know that you are going to the restroom and will return. Some hapless foreigners have been left in the restrooms as the bus and their bags continue the journey.

PLACES TO SEE

While visiting Guatemala, it is essential to see Antigua, Panajachel and Lake Atitlán, and Tikal. If there is more time, visit places like Quetzaltenango (Xela), Chichicastenango, and Lívingston.

Guatemala City

The capital is the major transportation hub both into and out of the country and within it. There is no need to linger in this sprawling city. There are very few sites worth visiting, it is generally dirty, and particular zones can be dangerous for the tourist. The city is famous for chaotic crowds and traffic pollution from the seemingly millions of smoke-blowing buses arriving and leaving. Most tourists only stay in Guate (as it's called by the locals) for a limited time and use it primarily as a transportation center to get to their next destination.

The cheaper and mid-range hotels are located in Zona 1, while the nicer hotels are in Zona 10. There are expensive restaurants and nightclubs in Zona Viva. There are some interesting museums in Zona 10 and 13, including the Museo Popol Vuh, which contains a good collection of Mayan and Spanish colonial art, and the Museo Ixchel, which has a wonderful display of the traditional arts and costumes of Guatemala's highland towns. Mayan artifacts can be found in the Museo de Arqueologia y Etnologia, and twentieth-century Guatemalan art in the Museo Nacional de Arte Moderno.

Antigua
This is one of the oldest and loveliest cities in the Americas. Antigua is about forty-five minutes by shuttle or private van from Guatemala City. Once the capital of Guatemala, until hit by devastating earthquakes in 1773, it has beautiful colonial buildings, colorful houses, and cobbled streets, set against the backdrop of three large volcanoes. Antigua is especially worth a visit during Semana Santa, when its streets are covered with bright

designs of flower petals and colored sawdust. It is also home to some impressive churches, including La Merced, the Iglesia de San Francisco, and the convent of Las Capuchinas, which is now a museum. A Sunday market is held in Parque Central. Because it is close to Guatemala City, idyllic, and peaceful—as

well as being home to many Spanish language schools—Antigua is probably the most visited tourist location in Guatemala.

Panajachel and Lake Atitlán

Sometimes jokingly called Gringotenango, because of the number of expatriates and foreign tourists who live and visit here, Panajachel is a beautiful and relaxing town to visit. Today, however, it is as popular with Guatemalans and other Central Americans as it is with the longtimers of North America. About half of the population of Panajachel remains non-Guatemalan and the town has become resortlike in its offerings, with many restaurants, tourist shops, and discos. The surrounding Lago de Atitlán (Lake Atitlán) is a breathtakingly scenic caldera lake—a water-filled collapsed volcanic cone. Panajachel became known in the 1960s as a sort of hippie haven with supposed mystical powers coming from vortex energy fields said to be located here. Today there are still many hippie types in Panajachel, making and selling jewelry and other crafts alongside the locals up and down the main streets. Panajachel is the home base for short boat trips to the smaller, mostly indigenous villages of Santiago Atitlán, Santa Catarina Palopo, and San Pedro La Laguna, all surrounding Lake Atitlán.

Tikal

The famous and impressive Mayan ruins of Tikal lie northwest of Flores in the jungle of El Petén. Tikal is among the world's most beautiful archaeological sites. The best example of Mayan

civilization at its peak, it lay forgotten and covered in thick jungle until the mid-nineteenth century. Plazas, an acropolis, pyramids, temples, and a museum can be found there. Many of the pyramids rise high above the tree canopy. There are many temples to climb in this immense hidden city, and the views are breathtaking. A wide range of animals can be seen in and around Tikal. These include howler and spider monkeys, coatimundi (a relation to the raccoon), parrots and other tropical birds—including the quetzal, after which the Guatemalan currency is named—and tree frogs. It is not generally known that Tikal was used to represent the rebel base in the classic *Star Wars* film!

Other Places

Chichicastenango is a highland town known for its famous Thursday and Sunday markets and traditional Mayan religious rites. Quetzaltenango, known by locals as Xela (pronounced "Shay-lah"), is the second-largest city in Guatemala. It is a good place to study Spanish, with numerous Spanish schools. Also noteworthy are the nearby villages, which are home to hot springs, small churches, and handicrafts. The central square is worth a visit, as the main meeting place for young and old, as is nearby San Francisco El Alto, the largest of all marketplaces in Guatemala.

Home to the Garífuna people of Guatemala is Lívingston, a tiny tropical island off the eastern coast with a distinctive culture made up of African, Mayan, and European elements. It is located near the Caribbean port of Puerto Barrios and is known for its laid-back charm and way of life, characterized by reggae music, drumming, coconut groves, brightly painted wooden buildings, and fishing. A boat ride on the nearby gorgeous Rio Dulce is an absolute must if you are visiting Lívingston.

HEALTH

There are two primary health risks about which to be concerned in Guatemala: contaminated water and food; and the moderate risk of contracting malaria in certain regions near the Pacific coast and in the rain forests of the Petén.

Contaminated water is the biggest cause of sickness in the country, and can lead to contraction of amoebas, parasites, and gastrointestinal infections, all of which are much more serious than simple traveler's diarrhea. Even if water appears to be sparkling clean, don't trust it. You should always drink bottled water that has been safely sealed. This is easily obtainable everywhere, but do check the seal. Most people also like to use bottled water to brush their teeth.

For the same reasons, eating from street vendors is usually not the best idea for visitors. Some people with tough stomachs are unaffected, but there is always a risk of food from street vendors being contaminated. In addition, first-time visitors should be careful about choosing uncooked food, such as salad and fruit, in certain restaurants because these may have been washed with contaminated water. In general, choose clean restaurants and ask how they wash their produce. Many restaurants, especially those catering to tourists, actually make this information public.

Regarding malaria, visitors should take an antimalarial medication if they plan to travel to areas of risk (especially the Petén).

The worst that happens to the majority of travelers to Guatemala is a case of diarrhea that can usually be cured with a couple of days of rest, plenty of bottled water, and bland foods. Pollution, and roads full of potholes and cracks, can also prove health hazards for some visitors.

In general, Guatemalans lack awareness about the dangers of HIV/AIDS (called SIDA in Guatemala). Although infection rates are low (1.1 percent in 2003) compared to some southern African countries (21.5–38.8 percent), there are very few government campaigns to educate people about HIV/AIDS. Guatemalans are generally unconcerned about the risks and are not likely to take safety precautions. Given this, visitors should behave sensibly and use precautionary measures in casual relationships.

There are many stray dogs in Guatemala, and rabies is endemic, so be careful. Don't feed the dogs and don't pet them, even if you feel sorry for them.

There are plenty of well-trained doctors in Guatemala and many who speak English. It is usually better to use a private hospital than a public one. Well-known North American and European prescription medicines are available in local pharmacies, and many do not require a prescription. However, the dosage or instructions may not be clearly stated.

SAFETY

Although Guatemala is often portrayed as violent, crime-ridden, and dangerous, most areas are relatively safe and the majority of tourists never have a problem. Some experienced travelers even claim that Guatemala is safer than many large U.S. and European cities. That said, it is important to stay away from isolated rural areas and from public gatherings where people seem to be upset, angry, or engaged in heated protests, which can turn violent. Petty crimes, such as pickpocketing or stolen luggage, and violence related to theft, such as muggings and carjacking, do occur, so visitors should be vigilant. If anything is stolen, it is highly unlikely that the thief will be caught or that your valuables will be returned.

Violence toward both foreigners and Guatemalans has increased in recent years, with women and girls being particularly targeted.

Women should avoid traveling to remote areas alone—it is safer to be accompanied by trustworthy Guatemalan. In general, it is prudent to take precautions by traveling in groups, leaving valuables locked in hotel safes if possible, and being especially careful in remote areas. Security escorts for tourist groups and security information are available from the Tourist Assistance Office of INGUAT (the Guatemalan Tourist Institute) in Guatemala City. The e-mail address is asistur@inguat.gob.gt.

Of growing concern is the rise of drug trafficking. Reportedly, Guatemala has overtaken Panama as the new Central American trafficking center in recent years. Controlled primarily by Colombian drug barons, the biggest trade is in cocaine, passing through on its way to the United States, followed by opium poppies, which are sold to Mexican traffickers for processing into heroin. In recent years, violence related to the drug trade has increased, especially along the Mexican border. Marijuana is also grown in Guatemala, but is used mainly for domestic consumption. All drugs are illegal in Guatemala, and those who are caught possessing, trafficking, or using any of the above drugs are dealt with severely, receiving long jail sentences or heavy fines.

DEALINGS WITH THE JUSTICE AND LEGAL SYSTEMS

Money laundering and general corruption continue to be serious problems. Historically, the police have been part of the problem in Guatemala, and many people are still wary of approaching them for assistance. Some believe the police force and the military to be involved with the drug trade, and there are questions about their participation in past civil war atrocities. In recent years, some police officers have been accused of orchestrating criminal gangs and engaging in other criminal activities. Overall, the Guatemalan police force and judicial system are weak and ineffective, and many officers are not sufficiently well trained. Most criminals know that they are unlikely to be caught or punished. It is easy to be impressed by the number of lawyers in Guatemala; however, many Guatemalans are also distrustful of the legal system, which is thought to be susceptible to bribes and corruption.

HELPFUL HINTS FOR TOURISTS

Guatemala is a photographer's dream, with its breathtaking scenery, diverse people, attractive, busy marketplaces, and colorful Maya clothing. However, expect mixed reactions from Guatemalans about being photographed. In some villages, you can expect locals to hide from the camera or show strong disapproval if they catch you taking photographs of them or their families. Be especially careful when taking pictures of children, as sometimes this has been misinterpreted by adults as being exploitative or leading to a potential kidnapping. Ask people for permission to take their picture; you will likely be asked for a couple of quetzals as payment in return.

It is fairly common in tourist locations to be pursued down the street by women and children trying to sell their handicrafts or textiles. This is typical, and should not be regarded as a nuisance. If you are interested, expect other sellers to approach you as well. If you are not interested, you can simply and firmly say "*No, gracias*" and walk away.

Often tourists who visit Guatemala are moved by what they see and want to help people, especially those from impoverished indigenous villages. Many students stay with a family while attending Spanish language schools and then continue to send money to their host family after they have left. There are many ways to help out, if you wish to do so, through Habitat for Humanity, Church and medical mission programs, and various other sound charitable organizations that offer services and resources to Guatemalans. It is important to remember that, especially for the Maya, education and preservation of their cultural heritage are priorities.

chapter eight

BUSINESS BRIEFING

As in any culture, if you don't know how the locals conduct business much can and usually does go wrong. In many Latin American countries (and Guatemala is no exception), forging good personal relationships is essential when doing business. Remember that building trust in relationships is the necessary precursor for successful business exchanges. For most businesspeople from the U.S.A. and Europe, this means that a greater effort than they are used to has to be made to build and maintain relationships with Guatemalan business partners. Do not expect to be concerned only with business, or always focused on the job in hand.

BUSINESS CULTURE AND ATTITUDES

In general, Guatemalans are open and straightforward, and tend to treat business partners as respected friends. They like to make others feel comfortable in both business and social situations and it is common to hear the

phrase, "*No tenga pena,*" which translates as "don't worry." Most Guatemalans strive for honesty, hard work, and personal honor in business deals, as these qualities are highly respected.

Guatemalans can, however, sometimes seem imprudent in their neglect of safeguards or precautionary measures at the planning stage, focusing instead on fixing the problem after the fact. Part of the reason for this attitude is the belief that disasters or problems are acts of God that cannot be prevented. To Westerners this looks like blind fatalism, but remember that this attitude is deeply rooted in Guatemalan culture, and is unlikely to be changed by a foreigner.

There are also some Guatemalan businesspeople who believe in the "prosperity theology" of certain of the neopentecostal sects, which holds that some people are wealthy because God wants them to be, and others are poor because they lack faith in Him.

It is important to have on-site Guatemalan representatives for any business venture, and it is generally expected that foreigners doing business in Guatemala will visit many times to demonstrate their sincere interest in the people and country. Guatemalan executives emphasize personal contacts with suppliers and partners and like to form long-lasting, trusting relationships. They are used to doing business with people from the United States, and higher executives and public officials can usually speak English. Guatemalans like to buy products from the United States, especially if they are inexpensive. Many manufacturing plants in the country are owned and managed by South Koreans.

Hierarchy and Status

Guatemalans tend to look for compromise and good relationships in the business setting. They build and focus on personal relationships with people at the same level, but it is clear that orders from above must be obeyed. Among equal-ranking employees, Guatemalans work well together and can be expected to function as a team, but this happens within a strict hierarchical framework. Most Guatemalans look to presenters, trainers, and teachers as the experts; speakers are generally expected to give formal presentations. The business environment is hierarchical and most companies are run by an autocratic boss. The hierarchy is not usually based on personal achievement but on social class, education, and family.

One way to increase your own status is to dress well, stay in expensive hotels, and discuss issues that demonstrate your intelligence—not to appear "superior" but rather as curious and open to learning about matters of importance to your hosts (business in Guatemala, its history, and so on).

Bureaucracy

Overall, Guatemalans do not like unpredictable and unclear situations in business. They typically emphasize rules, regulations, and controls in the workplace. For this reason, there can be a great amount of bureaucracy, especially in public and governmental offices. It is not uncommon to wait for many hours in a public office before being told that you are in the wrong place, or that you need to come back another day. Good luck if you find yourself needing some type of public document!

As a result, many foreign businesspeople can find themselves running into difficulties: restriction of materials, inadequate communication technology, and rigid working hours (the obligatory siesta, and not working at night). In such cases, remember that flexibility is key; don't personalize the situation, and don't get upset about practices that you can't change.

ADDRESSING AND GREETING PEOPLE

When greeting people in a business setting, it is very common for men and women to shake hands, although handshakes are generally gentler, longer, and more limp than in the West. It is appropriate to say "*mucho gusto*" (literally, "much pleasure") when shaking hands. Women sometimes pat each other's right forearm or shoulder instead. Male friends and female friends often hug and may lightly kiss each other on the cheek or pat each other's back. This is reserved, however, for people who know each other well. When introduced, it is important to smile and make direct eye contact, especially with Ladinos.

On your first introduction to a Guatemalan company or business, when you enter a room you should shake hands with everyone you meet and then again when departing. If you are returning to Guatemala, don't be surprised if people with whom you dealt most on previous visits greet you with a hug and a light kiss on the cheek.

Using titles when addressing people is a sign of respect, and is expected. Use their professional titles: a physician should be addressed as *Doctor/Doctora*, and anyone with a college degree can be addressed as *Licenciado/a*. Other titles are *Profesor/a, Arquitecto/a, Ingeniero/a, Maestro/a* (teacher), and so on. Otherwise, use Mr. (*Señor*), Mrs. (*Señora*), or Miss (*Señorita*), with surnames. You can also use the title without the last name (*Señora, Licenciado, Maestro*).

Most Guatemalans will have two surnames— their father's, which is commonly listed first, followed by their mother's. Only the father's surname is used when addressing someone. It is considered polite to speak softly and, of course, to engage in social conversation before business.

BUSINESS HOURS

For most commercial and industrial businesses, the hours are from 8:00 a.m. to 6:00 p.m., Monday through Friday. Plants and construction companies start at 7:00 a.m. and usually close between 4:00 and 5:00 p.m. Almost all banks open at 9:00 a.m. and close at 6:00 p.m. and automatic tellers usually close at 8:00 p.m., although some are open all night. Major credit cards are generally accepted by formal businesses and at tourist restaurants and sites. Businesses generally observe the holidays mentioned in Chapter 3. During *Semana Santa*, the week leading up to Easter, little or no business is conducted, and trying to do so may be viewed as insulting.

Many Guatemalan businesses close for siesta time, which occurs in the middle of the day for about two or three hours. It is generally not a good idea to schedule an appointment during this time because many businesspeople go home for lunch and relaxation and maybe a nap.

Guatemala is in the Central Standard Time zone, which means that it is one hour behind Eastern Standard Time. Because Guatemala does not observe daylight saving time, however, for about half of the year it is two hours behind Eastern Standard Time. Central Standard Time is six hours behind Greenwich Mean Time.

WOMEN IN BUSINESS

Although Guatemala is a traditionally male-dominated society, there are women who run businesses. Foreign businesswomen can expect to be treated respectfully by Guatemalan businessmen as long as the relationship remains focused on business. After work or at business outings, women may find themselves having to manage unwelcome attention from the same men; it is advisable to react politely and gracefully rather than aggressively, bearing in mind that a Guatemalan "come on" can seem cruder than is intended (see pages 59, 62).

DRESS CODE

For most business occasions, formal attire is appropriate. For men, a lightweight suit, and for women, a conservative dress or skirt and blouse are suitable. Women should dress conservatively to ward off any unwanted advances. Well-dressed individuals are appreciated, and casually dressed people may be viewed as disrespectful. For evening business functions, bring along a sweater or jacket as some cities can become chilly at night. During the rainy season, take an umbrella as there are frequent afternoon showers.

SETTING UP MEETINGS

Local contacts are absolutely crucial since a "cold-call" approach does not work well (there is no basis of a relationship, therefore no trust). If you don't have any Guatemalan contacts, you could arrange for a trade association, bank, or government agency to introduce you to Guatemalan businesspeople or companies. The first written correspondence with a company or business contact should be in Spanish, and then you can ask if it would be possible to continue in English. For appointments (*sitas*), you will need approximately two weeks' lead time in order to arrange the meeting, which will probably be in an office. The ideal time slots for meetings are late morning up until noon and then after 3:00 p.m. Although Guatemalans value time in a different way from North Americans or Europeans, they are generally punctual for business meetings.

MEETINGS

Remember that personal relationships are vital, and you should expect to spend a considerable amount of time in "small-talk" before turning to business. Chatting and inquiring about family is appreciated and almost expected. Good topics for conversation include soccer, places to visit in Guatemala, and details about your home town and country. Because Guatemalans are using this time to get to know you and determine if they can trust you, it is essential that you present a professional, formal, and intellectual image rather than being too open or too casual.

The majority of materials for meetings should be translated into Spanish, and business cards in Spanish are a good idea. When making presentations, concentrate on the content rather than attempting a persuasive sales pitch. In a business meeting, it is common for male guests to sit to the right of the host and women to the left.

NEGOTIATIONS

Business decisions in Guatemala are always made at the highest levels of authority, and chain of command is an important concept. Guatemalans generally try to match businesspeople with others of a similar rank. Because personal contacts and relationships are considered so important, it is usual to begin building the relationship before actual business has started. Likewise, foreign businesses need to offer the same availability in order to build trust with the Guatemalans.

When negotiating, it is important that no one becomes overly critical or too direct with regard to other people or companies (even competitors) as

this can be off-putting to Guatemalans, and can cause friction and discomfort in interactions. Guatemalans are inclined to bargain toughly. There is usually a lot of talking during negotiations and they may take a long time

Some visitors to Guatemala can be surprised by the level of touching and contact in business situations, and incorrectly assume that the Guatemalans are being insincere in order to close the business deal. However, this is not usually the case but rather a way of demonstrating that you are trusted and well-liked. Guatemalans also tend to stand very close to each other when talking—once you get to know people better, they are likely to stand close to you as well.

CONTRACTS

Civil law in Guatemala is based upon legislation and codification. The country has not yet accepted International Court of Justice (ICJ) jurisdiction. In rural Mayan areas, it is common for the indigenous people to follow their own time-honored customs and practices, which are respected above the law of the land.

Contracts in Guatemala are not regarded as sacrosanct. They are generally viewed only as papers, even if they are official and signed by a lawyer. Since breaking a contract is not likely to send anyone to jail, the importance of trust in the business relationship is paramount.

MALPRACTICE IN BUSINESS

Bribery, corruption, and fraudulent behavior are common in business and government in Guatemala. Some consider this to be a distortion of the traditional Guatemalan values of reciprocity, favors, and patronage. Although the current government promised to get rid of corruption in its election campaign, there has not been much progress in this area. For a foreigner it may be unclear how much difference a bribe would make in a business transaction and, if caught, how seriously it would be regarded. The best course is to operate ethically. The safest bet in business is to build honest relationships and treat people with respect and kindness, which may include offers of dinner and appropriate gifts. There are many unpredictable policies and business practices in Guatemala that have been created to benefit the small, 10 percent, wealthy minority. In business, this puts the large majority of Guatemalans at a disadvantage.

The Milder Side of Bribery and Corruption
International adoption of babies in Guatemala is
popular. A well-known adoption lawyer "hinted"
to a U.S. couple that he might be able to expedite
an adoption if the couple offered to pay for an
expensive, romantic dinner for him and his
girlfriend—"a helpful way to reward my efforts!"

BUSINESS ENTERTAINING

Business and social time frequently overlap, and it
is very common to be invited for a social outing
or dinner with business associates. In general,
Guatemalans tend to prefer business
breakfasts and lunches to dinners—
remember that the main meal of the
day is taken at noon rather than at
dinner. Business dinners are usually
lighter than lunches and typically
begin after 7:00 p.m. However, some
dinner parties actually don't begin until
closer to 10:00 p.m. Etiquette is important: when
offered a second helping, it is polite to decline at
first and then accept when your host insists.

Generally, Guatemalans don't like to talk
business while eating but instead wait until after
the meal is finished. Coffee typically follows the
meal, and is generally taken with milk and sugar.

This is usually when more in-depth business discussions occur.

If drinking alcohol, women should stick to wine or a mixed drink, because beer is considered a man's drink.

Guatemalans will know where excellent food is offered at reasonable prices. If you are hosting a meal, it would be appropriate to ask an executive's assistant to recommend a good restaurant.

GIFT GIVING AND FAVORS

Small gifts are commonplace in group business settings, but are not required for the first visit. These might be corporate merchandise such as pens, caps, or T-shirts. When meeting individuals, products or handicrafts from your home country would be appropriate.

It is not uncommon for Guatemalans to ask friends and business associates for favors. Don't be offended if asked, and unless it's completely unreasonable, try to grant the favor, as it will be expected. On the other hand, as a foreigner, it is not a good idea for you to ask too many favors. Guatemalans will generally grant your request, even if they don't want to, rather than be seen as impolite—but you don't want to be regarded as too demanding.

chapter **nine**

COMMUNICATING

LANGUAGE

The official language of Guatemala is Spanish, although there are at least twenty-three Mayan languages, in addition to Garífuna. Approximately 60 percent of the population speak Spanish, and the other 40 percent speak an indigenous language, as their mother tongue. Of the 40 percent, the majority will at least understand Spanish. However, in remote areas, and for Mayan women who mostly stay at home, the local Mayan dialect will be the primary language and people may have little or no understanding of Spanish. The most common Mayan language is K'iche', which is thought to have almost a million speakers. Other common Mayan languages include Mam, Q'eqchi', and Q'anjob'al.

In Spanish, there is the formal and the friendly or familiar pronoun "you." The formal "you" should be used when first meeting someone in Guatemala. However, Ladinos tend to use the familiar "you" (*tú* or *vos*) with almost everyone, and Mayans tend to use the formal "you" (*usted*) even within the family.

BODY LANGUAGE

Guatemalans are expressive, and it is typical to see people gesturing with their hands while they are talking. The spatial distance between two people in conversation tells you what type of relationship they have. For example, if they have just met, they are likely to maintain more distance, but if they are friends, the personal proximity is quite close—almost uncomfortably so for some foreigners. With foreigners, Guatemalans maintain a medium distance and personal space lessens as trust in the relationship increases. As we have seen, Guatemalans are apt to use the term *cariño* and be demonstratively affectionate with one another; however, it is not a good idea to use physical contact if you are a stranger. It communicates overfamiliarity, which may be seen as disrespectful. Too much physical touch by a foreign woman may be perceived by Guatemalan men as overtly sexual.

Among the Maya generally and some rural Ladinos, direct eye contact is considered disrespectful, which may be indicative of their lowly status in Guatemalan society. When meeting a Ladino, however, it is good to make direct eye contact initially.

There are two gestures that are considered obscene in Guatemala: the gesture where the tip of the thumb protrudes between the fingers of a closed fist, and the O.K. sign, which is the thumb and forefinger in the shape of a circle. Also, keeping your hands in your pockets while talking to someone is considered impolite in Guatemala.

HELLOS AND GOOD-BYES

Generally, Ladino Guatemalans will greet friends and relatives with a kiss on the cheek (if the recipient is a woman) and a hug. Ladino men are more likely to greet one another by embracing and patting each other on the back. If they don't know the person, men will typically shake hands with other men, and women will still kiss the cheek of a newly introduced woman. If the other person is older, it is important to stand up to greet or talk to them.

Mayan men are more likely to shake hands with one another than hug or kiss. They do not hug and kiss women friends either, but will usually avert their eyes and look down as a sign of respect. If they are wearing a hat or cap, they will typically take it off when talking to or greeting someone. Mayan women greet each other by extending their right arm and touching the other woman's arm in a "half-hug" fashion.

When meeting foreigners for the first time, Guatemalans will be a bit reserved and gently shake hands. Once they are better known and trusted, foreigners, like locals, are likely to receive a warm welcome with less distance, a hug, maybe a kiss on the cheek, and more emotion. Children are taught to kiss their relatives and friends of their parents in saying hello and good-bye. Guatemalans tend to wave good-bye with their hands raised in a fanlike fashion.

Generally, it is better to err on the side of formality when greeting Guatemalans. Do not casually use their first name when greeting someone unless they have already given you permission. Ladinos tend to be more casual and use the familiar "you" with almost everyone, unless they have only recently met you, while Maya are more likely to use the formal "you" even with family members.

CONVERSATION STYLE

Guatemalans will almost always ask about your family during an initial conversation. They will speak softly, which is considered to be polite, but this does not mean that they will not be expressive. They are likely to use their hands when talking and can be animated and dramatic when discussing something emotional. Ladino men especially seem to have a "way with words" and can be especially flattering to women to whom they are attracted.

Guatemalans are happy to talk about geography, history, and culture, but politics and the civil war are not topics you should broach—even if you hear people criticizing the government. Most Guatemalans do not like a confrontational style and you should avoid direct disagreement in conversation. They are likely to become silent and be offended. However, they themselves tend to interrupt others. Some Westerners are offended by what they feel is continual interruption when talking to Guatemalans—this is simply a difference of style, showing more comfort with overlaps while talking.

It is important to remain flexible and laid-back in all situations while in Guatemala, but especially when in conversation. If you try to steer a conversation toward a specific goal or outcome you will only end up frustrated. You may eventually get there, but it will be after a long period of time and with many non-sequiturs along the way. Personal interactions are what counts in Guatemala and this is reflected in the warm, genuine small talk that is exchanged.

Generally, too much direct eye contact when talking is seen as disrespectful.

HUMOR

Television is a major source of entertainment, and the Guatemalans enjoy watching comedy shows and cartoons. It is fair to say, however, that levity is not a feature of social life in Guatemala, though this of course depends on the individual. Puns, wordplay, and double-entendres (such as asking for a particular food to be passed at the table, where the food name is slang for a body part) are more common among younger people. In general, Guatemalans, especially the Maya, tend to be fairly serious, and some Mayan women even become embarrassed if they laugh too much.

THE MEDIA

There are several major newspapers in Guatemala that can be purchased for less than a quetzal at local roadside stands. The largest and most independent is *Prensa Libre*, a conservative, business-oriented publication that doesn't refrain from challenging the government. *Siglo Veintiuno*, its competitor, introduced modern investigative journalism to Guatemala. *La Hora* is a paper that comes out in the afternoons. The independent daily *elPeriódico* is liberal and left of center in its orientation. There are two tabloids. *Al Día* is bought for its sports section and many pictures, and *Nuestro Diario* is full of gossip, pictures, challenges to the government, and information about popular culture. There are other, smaller publications that are specific to particular areas, with a few written in English.

There are more than three hundred cable operators, plus several evangelical channels in Guatemala. The main channel, Canal 3, broadcasts the national news, with local news programs in larger cities. Most television channels in Guatemala are controlled by a private Mexican monopoly and offer entertainment rather than information.

Guatemala has several commercial and government-owned radio stations plus evangelical stations. The BBC World Service and the Voice of America have schedules and frequencies in Guatemala. Guatemalan women, especially in the rural areas, love soap operas, talk shows, and popular music, all of which are broadcast on the national radio stations. There are some stations with broadcasts in Mayan languages that focus on Mayan issues.

POSTAL SERVICES

Airmail is fairly reliable if you are sending something from Guatemala to Europe or the United States. However, receiving letters and packages while in Guatemala can prove much more difficult because the mail system is not reliable, and most packages are held in Guatemala City, where they are often tampered with or reported as lost. The safest (if expensive) way to receive packages is through courier services such as Federal Express, UPS, or DHL, all of which have offices in the larger cities. Letters can be received at the post office and picked up with proper identification. If not collected within one month, they are returned to the sender.

TELECOMMUNICATIONS

There are two main telephone service providers in Guatemala: Telgua and Telefónica. Both companies have telephone cards, but you have to ensure that you are dialing from the right type of phone. With Telefónica cards, you can dial from a private phone as long as it is a Telefónica phone; they also sell phone cards for use in their public phone booths. Telgua phones are everywhere, and can be used for international calls, but it is cheaper to find an Internet café or shop that offers an international phone service.

Cellular telephones are extremely popular in Guatemala and it is relatively inexpensive to buy one for use while visiting the country for extended or repeat visits. Almost every Guatemalan has a cell phone even if they don't have a landline at home.

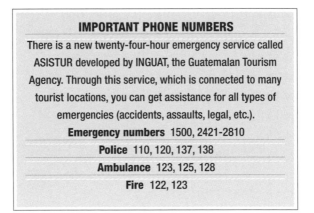

IMPORTANT PHONE NUMBERS

There is a new twenty-four-hour emergency service called ASISTUR developed by INGUAT, the Guatemalan Tourism Agency. Through this service, which is connected to many tourist locations, you can get assistance for all types of emergencies (accidents, assaults, legal, etc.).

Emergency numbers 1500, 2421-2810

Police 110, 120, 137, 138

Ambulance 123, 125, 128

Fire 122, 123

The country code for Guatemala is 502, and it is now necessary to use an additional digit at the beginning of the typical seven-digit phone number: 2 for Guatemala City numbers; 5 for cell phone numbers; 6 for the suburbs of Guatemala City; and 7 for outside Guatemala

City. To dial abroad from Guatemala, dial 00 followed by the country code. Most people answer the phone in Guatemala by saying, "*Bueno*," and waiting for your response.

COMPUTERS

Internet cafés can be found in the large cities, many smaller towns, and, more recently, even in remote areas. It is important to know where to find the @ ("*aroba*") symbol on the Spanish keyboard. Usually, it will appear if you press "alt 6" and then "4" on the number pad. Most Guatemalans do not have computers at home.

CONCLUSION

An American student who has twice stayed in the country summed it up as follows:

> "Guatemala is hard to explain. It's got a little bit of everything—city, country, beach. The people of Guatemala are as difficult to describe as the layout of the country. They are in the middle of the past and present, some are disenfranchised, but many I met were very motivated and connected to one another.
>
> Guatemala can be a hard place to be because life there holds many challenges:

poverty, history of a corrupt government system, tendency toward alcoholism in men, strong women who are taught to obey and manage at the same time. Guatemala isn't the most clean or easy to live in place, but the people I met had some serious heart.

The appeal of Guatemala may be due to the combination of Latino ideology (*familismo*, *simpatico*) and the syncretism of the Ladino and Mayan cultures that come together to form the country; but whatever it is, Guatemala is at once beautiful and hard."

The most lasting impression of this fascinating country comes from the vitality and resilience of the Guatemalan people, who are warm, friendly, and welcoming, despite enduring years of terror and abuse in the thirty-six-year civil war.

Guatemala today is a unique combination of ancient Mayan culture, Spanish colonialism, and Western influences, mainly from the U.S.A. There are few places left where one can see an indigenous people such as the Maya so committed to revitalizing their identity, traditions, and customs.

Both Ladinos and Maya are renowned for their *fiestas*, traditional costumes, and lively marketplaces. Family life and personal relationships are of utmost importance to them. As a visitor, it may take you a while to build trust or be successful in business with the Guatemalans, but once you have earned their friendship, your future relations will have a solid foundation.

Be ready for early morning firecrackers, chicken buses, flexible schedules, and lots of tortillas, and you will truly learn to love the eccentricities and flavors of Guatemalan culture. Guatemala's natural beauty and its determined people lie in great contrast to its brutal history. The Guatemalans are resolute in their quest for a better country, and after their visit, most foreigners will want the same for their new Chapín friends.

Appendix: Some Noteworthy Guatemalans

Ricardo Arjona

Arjona is an acclaimed singer, songwriter, and composer with an international reputation. His music incorporates political and social messages. It is usually classified as Spanish Pop, although much of his work varies widely. He has been living in Mexico since the late 1980s.

Miguel Ángel Asturias

A writer and diplomat, Asturias was awarded the Nobel Prize for Literature in 1967 for his literary work highlighting the indigenous people of Guatemala. Asturias was active in politics throughout his life and during his exile from Guatemala became well-known for his novel *Mulata*. In 1966 he was appointed Ambassador to France and in the same year was awarded the Lenin Peace Prize.

Justo Rufino Barrios

Regarded as a national hero for his liberal, far-reaching reforms, Barrios was president of Guatemala from 1873 to 1885. He instituted freedom of the press and of religion and tried to unite Central America. He brought the first telegraph lines and railroads to Guatemala and set up a public school system. His portrait is on the five-quetzal bill, and Puerto Barrios is named after him.

Myrna Mack Chang

Mack was an anthropologist, well-known for her work with Mayan rural communities, who suffered during the

Guatemalan civil war. Born in Guatemala into a wealthy, mixed Ladino-Chinese family, she studied anthropology in the United Kingdom. In 1990, she was brutally stabbed to death by a military death squad associated with the Guatemalan government. This assassination was reportedly in retaliation for her exposing the destruction of indigenous rural communities during the civil war. Mack's was the first human-rights case to go to the courts during the civil war, and paved the way for other human-rights violations to be brought to justice.

Rigoberta Menchú Tum

She is known chiefly for her book *I, Rigoberta Menchú*, published in the early 1980s, which detailed the human-rights abuses committed against the Mayan people during the civil war in Guatemala and brought the world's attention to the situation. In 1992, she was awarded the Nobel Peace Prize for her work in social justice and the rights of indigenous peoples.

Carlos Mérida

Mérida was a renowned painter (1891–1984). He lived and traveled in Europe after attending art school in Guatemala, and eventually settled in Mexico, where he became one of Mexico's first nonfigurative artists. He was well-known for his murals in both Mexico and Guatemala and today his paintings can be found in many international museums.

José Efraín Ríos Montt

Infamous and controversial, Montt was the dictator of Guatemala and, after being ousted in a coup, head of Congress. During the early 1980s, his military regime carried out the most violent atrocities of the entire thirty-six-year civil war, including widespread massacres, rape, and torture against the Maya. During his rule, the government targeted thousands of Mayas who were thought to be sympathizers and supporters of the guerrilla movement. Some critics label his campaigns deliberate genocide against the Mayan people. In the 2003 presidential election, Montt, as a candidate for the Guatemalan Republican Front (FRG), was defeated by Óscar Berger.

Carlos Ruíz

Also known as "El Pescadito" (the little fish), Ruiz is a famous soccer player in Major League Soccer in the U.S.A. and on the Guatemalan national team. He was the lead scorer for the Guatemalan team, helping them to qualify for the 2006 FIFA World Cup. Currently he plays for FC Dallas, one of the Major League Soccer teams in the United States based in Texas.

Further Reading

Benz, Stephen Connoly. *Guatemalan Journey*. Austin, TX: University of
Texas Press, 1996.

Fischer, Edward F., and R. McKenna Brown. *Maya Cultural Activism in
Guatemala*. Austin, TX: University of Texas Press, 1996.

Forsyth, Susan, John Noble, and Conner Gorry. *Lonely Planet Guatemala*.
Oakland, CA: Lonely Planet Publications, 2004.

Menchú, Rigoberta. *I, Rigoberta Menchú—An Indian Woman in Guatemala*.
New York: Verso, 1982.

O'Kane, Trish. *In Focus: Guatemala—A Guide to the People, Politics and
Culture*. New York: Interlink Books, 2000.

Schlesinger, Stephen, and Stephen Kinzer. *Bitter Fruit: The Story of the
American Coup in Guatemala*. (Revised and expanded.) Boston: Harvard
University Press, 2005.

Shea, Maureen E. *Culture and Customs of Guatemala*. Westport, CT:
Greenwood Press, 2001.

Tedlock, Dennis. *Popol Vuh: The Definitive Edition of the Mayan Book of the
Dawn of Life and the Glories of Gods and Kings*. (Revised and expanded.)
New York: Touchstone, 1996.

Tooley, Michelle. *Voices of the Voiceless: Women, Justice, and Human Rights
in Guatemala*. Scottdale, PA: Herald Press, 1997.

Whatmore, Mark, and Iain Stewart. *Guatemala: The Rough Guide*.
New York: Penguin Books, 2002

In-Flight Spanish. New York: Living Language, 2001.

Spanish. A Complete Course. New York: Living Language, 2005.

Fodor's Spanish for Travelers (CD Package). New York: Living Language,
2005.

culture smart! **guatemala**

Index

culture smart! guatemala

Acknowledgement

I am grateful for the contributions provided by my dear Guatemalan friends, Gabriela and Jose.